I0160885

More Nuggets From Heaven

Written and Complied
By

Rayola Kelley

Hidden Manna Publications

More Nuggets from Heaven

ISBN: 978-1-7347503-6-2

The book has been printed in the USA.

Except where otherwise indicated, all Scripture quotations in this book are taken from the King James Version of the Bible.

Hidden **M**anna **P**ublications
P.O. Box 3572
Oldtown, ID 83822
www.gentleshepherd.com

Facebook:
https://www.facebook.com/HiddenMannaPublications/

Dedication

To

John Wulff,
a faithful friend,
and brother in the Lord.

You have proven generous in
your friendship, support, and service,
which is truly inspiring and greatly appreciated.

Table of Contents

Introduction

The one truth we know about God's storehouse of treasures is that it is inexhaustible. Since God is eternal, no one can begin to drain His various resources. Whether it is a matter of blessings, promises, or gifts, the veins in which spiritual treasures flow from His throne are unstoppable and endless.

This is the second book unveiling the treasures that have graced my life. In the first book, I so enjoyed exploring the spiritual treasure chest of His truths as I considered and appreciated the simple, yet beautiful gems that I had collected through the years. It delighted my soul to once again examine the treasures that had touched and enriched my life with a bit of heaven.

Unlike the first book where the nuggets had come my way as special gifts, I had to dig for the treasures in this book. We know that great treasures can also be found in the ground, hidden and invisible to the eye. For this reason, such treasures require us to search and dig in places to find veins that harbor these rich resources. For me, I had to tap into the recesses of my mind to remember my encounter with past jewels, dig in books and diaries to find valuable treasures long hidden or forgotten, search through devotions and hymnals to snatch gems, wade through materials obtained through the Internet to polish those bits of treasures that had become tarnished through time, and pan various other resources to compile this book.

The book in your hands contains quotable sayings, legends, poems, prayers, and stories which go back as far as Polycarp (70 A.D. to 156 A.D.) into the Puritan era, to the present. Some have been lifted out of pages yellowed by time after being covered by the dust of indifference and tarnished by the darkness of the ages, to once again allow their reflective beauty to grace and challenge our lives. As in the previous book, I have marked the gems that God has personally graced my life with by my initials, *RJK.* Besides lacing the book with Scriptures to highlight the subject, I have also attempted to mark the sources in which I have discovered some of these treasures. (See the Bibliography for clarification.) Unless otherwise noted, the legends and stories that have been told in this book are based on my personal recollection of when I first read or heard them.

As you consider this treasure chest, you will see names that are controversial, but the message rings with truths that have to be discerned. As the Bible states, you can do nothing against the truth, and works will follow those who serve Him. You will realize that some of these riches have been passed down through twenty centuries by those who dared to carry them in their bosoms. These brave souls maintained the integrity of these treasures during times when thieves threatened to rob them, murderers waited to kill them for possessing such treasures, and the oppressive and hateful environment of destruction threatened to take them down into a pit of despair. It is for this reason that these treasures are priceless. It is because they are often hidden by the protective and abiding hand of God that they have survived through oppressive ages to once again be brought to the full light so others can enjoy their simple beauty.

The journey to discover these gems proved to be quite rewarding to me, but it reminded me that there is a cost to not only possess these nuggets, but to find them. The search can take you in many directions to explore different terrains, causing the seeker to become somewhat overwhelmed and occasionally weary. However, this is part of the enrichment. For me, my understanding was enlarged, my faith confirmed, and my joy at discovering His incredible treasures once again was revived by those who have striven to preserve them.

My prayer is that the treasures in this book will also revive and enlarge the reader to become a treasure seeker of the eternal riches of heaven. To discover such treasures will not only enrich one's life, but will also enlarge the value of the eternal inheritance that will be fully unveiled in the ages to come.

A Matter of Salvation

A man by the name of Tertullian made this statement, "Every soul is considered as having been born in Adam until it has been reborn in Christ. Moreover, it is unclean until it has been regenerated."

Salvation lies at the heart of God and should be the consistent theme of every Christian. Even though you can read the works of Tertullian and see that he confronted the issues of his day, the concerns and challenges for the saints of God remain the same—the salvation of man. Clearly, man in his unregenerate state, remains unchanged towards the matters of righteousness and God's attitude towards sin has never changed regardless of the times. As a result, man's soul hangs in the balance.

Tertullian who lived from 160-230 A. D. was an ordained presbyter. He wrote numerous apologies in regard to the culture of his times as well as works that exposed heresies. It has been my goal to bring a contrast between the early works of Christians in light of the Christianity that is presently being promoted.

Various works from these early Christians will be presented throughout this book to bring contrast and enlightenment. As you will see, the truth is always the truth regardless of the time or generation. In some instances, their statements are miniature sermons. I found most of these statements in two very important resource books. They are: *The Golden Treasury of Patristic Quotations (GPQ),* compiled by I. D. E. Thomas, and *A Dictionary of Early Christian Beliefs (DCB),* edited by David W. Bercot. It is clear that much time and energy were put forth in these books to bring to life those who influenced the early Church. It is my hope that each of these nuggets from above will reflect a valuable contrast.

The above statement from Tertullian came from *The Golden Treasury of Patristic Quotations (GPQ),* pg. 250.

******

- It is man who complicates a matter, and God's wisdom that clarifies it. Sadly, man is forever adding onto the simplicity of Christ. You wonder why people must complicate such matters. It is easy to answer such a question. It is a matter of unbelief. They simply cannot or will not accept or receive the simple message of salvation.

-RJK

But I fear, lest by any means, as the serpent beguiled Eve through his subtilty, so your minds should be corrupted from the simplicity that is in Christ (2 Corinthians 11:3).

- If men can get to heaven by being good, then the death of Christ is the worst waste in human history.

-Dr. Toussaint

- Wanna know if Jesus Christ is THE ONLY WAY to heaven??? .....Ask the lost souls in hell!!

- unknown

- As believers, we all start out like Rahab, undesirable and unlikely as a candidate for salvation. But, by faith, we believed the Gospel, securing a new life, knowing that we will not perish in our sins. We are now identified to the new covenant established by the blood of Jesus.

-RJK

But God hath chosen the foolish things of the world to confound the wise; and God hath chosen the weak things of the world to confound the things which are mighty (1 Corinthians 1:27).

- I will not glory because I am righteous, but because I am redeemed; not because I am clear of sin, but because my sins are forgiven.

  -Ambrose of Milan
  GPQ, pg. 105

- Do not doubt whether it is possible: for He that on this sacred Golgotha saved the robber after only one hour of believing, the same will save you, if you believe.

  -Cyril of Jerusalem
  GPQ, pg. 97

And he said unto Jesus, Lord, remember me when thou comest into thy kingdom. And Jesus said unto him, Verily I say unto thee, To day shalt thou be with me in paradise (Luke 23:42-43).

******

The Love of Christ

Here is love,
that God sent His Son,
His Son that never offended,
His Son that was always His delight.
Herein is love, that He sent Him to save sinners;
to save them by bearing their sins,
by bearing their curse, by dying their death,
and by carrying their sorrows.
Here is love, in that while we were yet enemies,
Christ died for us;
yes, here is love, in that while we were yet without strength,
Christ died for the ungodly.

-John Bunyan
(HFC, pg. 356)

But God commendeth his love toward us, in that while we were yet sinners, Christ died for us. Much more then, being now justified by his blood, we shall be saved from wrath through him (Romans 5:8-9).

******

A New Status

Jesus is clear that a man must be born again to enter the kingdom of heaven (John 3:3, 5). A person must have a new heart and spirit that identifies him or her to the spiritual and heavenly life. Such a life comes from above, from outside of any attempts of a person. It is truly a gift of God.

We are told that with this new life we are given a new inheritance. In fact, we have been endowed with the seal of the Holy Spirit to identify us to this inheritance. This brings us to the fact that we have a new status as well. The status is that of being a child of God.

The Bible tells us that as believers we have been adopted into a new family. America's adoption policy points to someone being an orphaned or abandoned and brought from outside of a family to be given the same status and rights as a child who was born into the family. However, in the days of the Apostle Paul, adoption had a different take on it. According to H. A. Ironside's commentary on Galatians every child born into the Roman Empire possessed the same status as a servant or slave. It was only when the father took the intended heir to the courts of the land and officially adopted him or her that the child could be assured of an inheritance.

When you consider adoption from this perspective, it brings more clarity to what it means to be adopted into the family of God. Every person is born into the Adamic race. As a result, each individual possesses the status of a slave to sin. However, God provided the necessary documentation of adoption when Jesus died on the cross to redeem each of us. As believers, we need to not only embrace our new status by faith, but we must strive to reach the heights of excellence in order to properly embrace our glorious inheritance.

For ye have not received the spirit of bondage again to fear; but ye have received the Spirit of adoption, whereby we cry, Abba, Father (Romans 8:15).

- I look upon this world as a wrecked vessel. God has given me a lifeboat and said to me: Moody save all you can.

  -Dwight L. Moody

- Salvation is a helmet, not a nightcap."

  -Vance Havner

And take the helmet of salvation, and the sword of the Spirit, which is the word of God (Ephesians 6:17).

- God can take an insignificant branch like Abraham and produce fruit a thousand-fold. He can take a small branch like David and produce a strong nation. He also took an unlikely branch in the form of His Son, and provided salvation for all who will believe.

  -RJK

- The salvation in which we believe is proved not from clever reasoning, but from the Holy Scriptures.

  -Cyril of Jerusalem
  GPQ, pg. 243

- For many people in our churches these days, salvation is all in their minds. This will result in their missing heaven by eighteen inches, because God's salvation has never gotten down from their heads into their hearts, where Christ can become their life. They know the verses, but they do not know Him; whom to know is life eternal.

  -Paris Reidhead
  FRG, pg. 19

That if thou shalt confess with thy mouth the Lord Jesus, and shalt believe in thine heart that God hath raised him from the dead, thou shalt be saved (Romans 10:9).

- Stand still, and see the salvation of God. He knows the way, and He will direct thee in it if thou cry unto Him.

-Charles Spurgeon
(FCB, pg. 59)

- Most of us are thronging Him—just like the crowd. . . It is easy to throng the Lord and never touch Him. A great many people in the churches, and perhaps a great many seeking Him, coming close to Him, but never actually touching Him. In this matter of eternal importance, coming close is not enough. It is like missing a train. . . You may miss it by one minute— and that's pretty close— but you have lost the train. . . It is gone, and you are left behind. Thronging saves nobody. Coming near to Jesus will not bring healing. We have to touch Him for ourselves.

-Peter Marshall
(JMM, pg. 185)

- Surprisingly, over the years, I have heard many Christians talk about Jesus' deliverance in terms of circumstances, but some of these individuals have failed to realize Jesus' true deliverance is not of a physical nature, but of a spiritual one. God's love did not reach through circumstances to save people from unpleasant conditions. Rather, He reached through the darkness of men's souls with His light to save them from the ways of death. This light is the very life of Jesus.

-RJK

In him was life; and the life was the light of men (John 1:4)

******

There is Always Tomorrow

We humans have a tendency to put off today what fails to catch our fancy or excitement. We always perceive that we have tomorrow. It is true that some matters can be put off until tomorrow, but there are other matters that should not be put aside because the opportunity to ensure a beneficial outcome may be narrow and limited. And, there are still some matters that will ultimately reveal the folly and destruction of such procrastination.

I remember the story about a young couple who came to an evangelistic meeting. As they listened to the message, they were almost persuaded by the Holy Spirit and the urgent exhortations of the evangelist to come forward and give their lives to Jesus. However, they reasoned that since they were young, they always had tomorrow to resolve such an issue. After all, death seemed far away from them in light of the strength of their youth. In their minds, they had much life to live and embrace before the unmerciful grip of death enveloped them.

They happily walked out of the meeting to enjoy some ice skating on the frozen lake. As they gleefully enjoyed the folly of their youth, the unpredictable claws of death reached up and snatched them as the ice broke beneath their feet. They were pulled down into the icy waters of death to face an eternity without Jesus.

Augustine said, "God has promised forgiveness to your repentance; but He has not promised tomorrow to your procrastination". Basil the Great stated that God says "today"; the devil says "tomorrow". It is clear that the matters regarding life that must never be put off are those that involve eternity.

(For he saith, I have heard thee in a time accepted, and in the day of salvation have I succoured thee: behold, now is the accepted time; behold, now is the day of salvation) (2 Corinthians 6:2).

❖ Sometimes a sinner parlays with his Savior, wishing he could have a little of the honor of his salvation, wanting to keep some favorite sin and amend the humbling terms of grace. But Jesus will be all in all, and the sinner must be nothing at all.

-Charles Spurgeon

❖ It is little wonder then that many are disillusioned with Christianity. They have yet to realize that salvation is *not* a plan, *not* in scripture verses, *not* in ordinances and *not* in a scheme of theology. Salvation is *not* a decision and *not* a pronouncement of an evangelist, a pastor or a teacher. . . Salvation is a *Person*—Jesus Christ.

-Paris Reidhead
FRG, pg. 19

Verily, verily, I say unto you, The hour is coming, and now is, when the dead shall hear the voice of the Son of God: and they that hear shall live. For as the Father hath life in himself; so hath he given to the Son to have life in himself (John 5:25-26).

❖ The primary work of salvation is not a matter of saving us from hell; rather, it is the complete work of Christ to reconcile us back into a relationship with God.

-RJK

❖ *Jesus* save me now—It is He
Jesus *saves* me now—It is His work to save.
Jesus saves *me* now—I am the one to be saved.
Jesus saves me *now*—He is doing it every moment.

-Hannah Whitall Smith
(CHL, pg.53)

❖ The follower of Jesus makes the salvation of the soul the first object in his holy ministry of love.

-Andrew Murray

❖ There is true conversion where there have been covenant transactions between God and the soul.

-Matthew Henry

❖ Praying people are the only people who have influence with God, the only people to whom God connects Himself and His Gospel.

-E. M. Bounds
(WOP, pg. 44)

Praying always with all prayer and supplication in the Spirit, and watching thereunto with all perseverance and supplication for all saints (Ephesians 6:18)

******

My dear friend, Maureen Human, physically lived through a Job's experience for the better part of a year. I encouraged her to write some of her feelings during her ordeal. Throughout this book you will be graced with some of her thoughts. As I followed her writings, it was almost like watching a graceful phoenix rising out of the ashes of devastation. I could see the seriousness of her meditation as well as the redefining of what she deemed important and significant. It was through her eyes that I was reminded that beauty is so often discovered in simplicity.

Folly is that in which we
deceive ourselves to be
more than who we are!
Only He who has paid
the price can save us
from ourselves.

-Maureen Human

- I must be saved from the guilt of sin, the power of sin, the punishment of sin, and ultimately from the very being of sin. God hath said it: "Thou shalt be saved." I believe it. I shall be saved, I am saved. Glory be to God for ever and ever.

-Charles Spurgeon

For whosoever shall call upon the name of the Lord shall be saved (Romans 10:13).

- The nature of Christ's salvation is woefully misrepresented by the present-day evangelist. He announces a Savior from Hell rather than a Savior from sin. And that is why so many are fatally deceived, for there are multitudes who wish to escape the Lake of Fire who have no desire to be delivered from their carnality and worldliness."

-A.W. Pink

- If anyone has hoped in Christ as a Man lacking a mind, he is truly mindless and is quite unworthy of being saved. That which was not assumed has not been healed; but that which is united to God, the same is saved. If only half of Adam fell, then what is assumed and saved may also be only half; but if the whole of Adam fell, it must be united as whole to Him that is born, in order to be wholly saved.

  -Gregory of Nazianzus
  GPQ, pg. 242

- No one has the right to think themselves a child of God unless they have the witness of the Spirit to the new birth!

  -John Wesley

He that believeth on the Son of God hath the witness in himself; he that believeth not God hath made him a liar; because he believeth not the record that God gave of his Son (1 John 5:10).

******

The Reality of Sin

It is hard to understand the devastation sin works upon our lives for we live in the constant state of it. We do not see how it mars our potential, causes us to love its very darkness, fiercely guard its wicked ways, justify its incessant wrongs, and make its cruelties right and acceptable in our own sight.

However, we must remember sin mars, ruins, and devastates every aspect of our lives. There is nothing sacred from its far reaching tentacles of perversion, wretchedness, and destruction. In fact, we get a glimpse of how sin mars that which is pure and righteous. All we have to do is consider Jesus and Him crucified. The perfect Son and sinless Lamb of God was so marred by the affront of others' sin upon His physical body that He became undesirable to the onlookers who mocked and despised Him.

Sin's ability to mar everything perfect, innocent, and sincere was brought to the forefront by a legend surrounding the painting of the "Last Supper." I admit my exact recollection of the time period may somewhat vary, but the intent remains the same. According to the legend, Da Vinci searched for men whom he felt would best portray Jesus and His disciples. For example, the man he used to portray Jesus was 19 years old, still untouched by the wicked influences of the world.

The artist was diligent in his search for each person who would properly represent each disciple. However, he hit a snag when it came to Judas Iscariot. He wanted someone who looked liked a criminal of the worst type. Such a man would have to reveal how the ways of the world could truly destroy the countenance and soul of a person's very being.

It was not until almost five years after he started the project that he finally located his Judas. He found him incarcerated by the justice system. He secured permission to paint the criminal as the notorious Judas. After six months of painstaking observation, he felt he had captured the essence of the man's deviant character on canvas. He signaled the guard to usher the man away for the last time.

Before the guard had escorted the man to the door, the criminal broke away and rushed to the painter. He cried, "Da Vinci do you not recognize me?" The painter looked at him intently and stated that to his recollection he had never seen him before his present encounter with him. It was at that time the criminal cried, "Oh, have I fallen so far, five years ago you painted me as Jesus!"

As many were astonied at thee; his visage was so marred more than any man, and his form more than the sons of men (Isaiah 52:14).

❖ It has been well said that, "Earthly cares are a heavenly discipline" But they are even something better than discipline,—they are God's chariots, sent to take the soul to its high place of triumph...Everything becomes a "chariot of salvation" when God rides upon it.

-Hannah Whitall Smith
(CHL, pg. 234)

- Conversion is the attitude of correcting wrong things in the day to day Christian life.

  -Paris Reidhead
  FRG, pg. 19

- How important is the Gospel? The good news of the Gospel is that man can be saved from his spiritual plight of oppression and his state of separation from the essence of all life, God.

  -RJK

- Salvation truly goes back to genuine repentance.

  -Jeannette Haley

In those days came John the Baptist, preaching in the wilderness of Judaea, And saying, Repent ye: for the kingdom of heaven is at hand (Matthew 3:1-2).

- If God's today be too soon for thy repentance, then tomorrow may be too late for His acceptance.

  -William Secker
  (PDC, pg. 294)

- By denying forgiveness they remove the incentive to repentance.

  -Ambrose of Milan
  (GPQ. Pg. 106)

- What is conviction of sin? It is that state of the mind and heart when the individual takes the sides with God against himself. Conviction is the work of the Spirit of God in the human heart that causes the individual to realize something of the enormity of the crime that he has committed against God.

  -Paris Reidhead
  (FRG, pg 66)

- It is not enough to hear the Gospel; we must receive the light of that Gospel. It is not enough to quote the Gospel; we must walk in the light of its incredible hope. It is not enough to preach the

Gospel; we must live the Gospel in the resurrection power and authority of the Son of God.

-RJK

But if our gospel be hid it is hid to them that are lost: In whom the god of this world hath blinded the minds of them who believe not, lest the light of the glorious gospel of Christ, who is the image of God, should shine unto them (2 Corinthians 4:3-4).

❖ There is no way to find our life but as Jesus did—in giving it up for the salvation of others.

-Andrew Murray

❖ We therefore, who have been called by His will in Christ Jesus, are not justified by ourselves, neither by our wisdom or understanding or piety, not by the works we have wrought in holiness of heart, but by faith by which Almighty God has justified all men from the beginning.

-Clement of Rome

******

A Clear Vision

If you are like me, I love to read about the lives of missionaries. Reading about the works of David Brainerd with the Native Americans, William Carey and Amy Carmichael among the people of India, Adoniram Judson in Burma, and Hudson Taylor in China to name a few, always inspires my soul and causes my spirit to consider the impossible and the eternal.

Many of these missionaries faced tremendous hardships such as the loss of their spouses and children in a foreign land. Some were imprisoned, as well as shunned and mocked by Christians who did not understand their dedication or who were seized by jealousy.

As I read about these people lives, I marvel at their willingness to risk it all. In studying their lives there is one consistent factor that enabled these stout pilgrims to face the unknown and risk everything to tread where no one else had walked before, and that was a vision for the lost souls that Jesus had died for.

One such missionary that tread where no other Protestant missionary had previously been, was a Welshman by the name of Robert Reid Kalley. Even though his name is relatively unknown, he was used mightily by God in Madeira, Funchal, and Brazil. He was a doctor who not only sacrificially offered his services to better the lives of those who were suffering, but he also offered that which would bring healing to their souls. He not only preached the Gospel but established schools in which he could disciple the natives in the ways of God. As a point of edification, he wrote Christian pamphlets and translated such books as *Pilgrim Progress* into the people's native language. His efforts not only prepared those converted under him to stand in trying times, but to share the life-changing message with others.

Dr. Kalley set off to Madeira without any official backing. He had a calling that he could not nor would he ignore. He made this statement, "It will be my duty to lift up a standard for the truth. I would willingly do so at once...for I do not regard the license from any body of men at all essential before preaching the glad tidings of salvation to perishing souls. The message is God's, not man's, and appears to me so plainly given in the Word that I would have no hesitation on that score."

He was greatly persecuted by the priests of the Catholic Church. He even spent time in prison in Madeira, and barely escaped with his life. The religious conflict was not limited to the Catholic priests that viewed him as a threat, but he also found himself embroiled in conflict over doctrinal disagreement among the religious organization that he was associated with.

Dr. Kalley knew his calling. He was determined to keep his vision clear. He wrote about it in his diary dated April 8, 1855. "Leaving Britain would have been unbearable but for the feeling that it was to carry words of peace from God to reveal to creatures and with the hope of seeing fruit for our trials and labours for ever. The object in view is worth labouring for, suffering for, and it is worth spending life in pursuit of it."

There are many that are interested in their biological lineage, but how many of us know our spiritual lineage. It would be safe for us to say that our lineage goes back to missionaries such as Paul. But, what other missionaries would we find in our different lineages who consecrated their lives so that we could be part of the rich heritage established on the cross by Jesus Christ?

How then shall they call on him in whom they have not believed? and how shall they believe in him of whom they have not heard? And how shall they hear without a preacher (Romans 10:14)?

The Work of the Cross

- The cross of Christ lies at the core of the greatest story ever told and the revelation of the greatest life that was ever lived. It will remain in the journals of eternity as the ladder that reached heaven, the bridge that closed the great gap between God and man, and an ugly instrument that revealed the glory, power, and love of God in light of sacrifice, suffering, and death.

  -RJK

- How can we expect to find Jesus if we do not seek Him in the states of His earthly life, in loneliness and silence, in poverty and suffering, in persecution and contempt, in annihilation and the cross?

  -Fenelon

- The cross did away with man and put Christ in his place. When you have found this godly perspective, you can begin to see in a Christ-centered way.

  -Manfred Haller
  (CA, pg. 41)

- I have no intention to depart in the smallest degree from the main principles on which I have acted in the past. My only hope for the permanent deliverance of mankind from misery, either in this world or the next, is the regeneration or remaking of the individual by the power of the Holy Ghost through Jesus Christ. But in providing for the relief of temporal misery I reckon that I am only making it easy where it is now difficult, and possible where it is now all but impossible, for men and women to find their way to the Cross of our Lord Jesus Christ.

-William Booth

❖ The waters of the world are bitter like those at Marah as described in Exodus 15:22-25. However, a tree was cast into it to make it sweet. This is what God has done with the cross of Jesus. He has cast it into the bitter waters of this present world so we can freely drink from the wells of salvation. As we partake of this life, we will know the sweetness of redemption and communion.

-RJK

Therefore with joy shall ye draw water out of the wells of salvation (Isaiah 12:3).

❖ The cross is the chief mark of the Christian as it was of Christ.

-Andrew Murray

❖ People are needed in the pulpit, as well as in the pew, who are bold enough to take up and firm enough to sustain the consecrated cross.

-E. M. Bounds
(WOP, pg. 114)

❖ From all appearances, Jesus, Peter, and Paul's lives would appear as a waste since they were offered up by the age in which they lived. However, heaven does not see it that way. In spite of the humanness they had to overcome, they finished the course set before them. For Jesus, the course included the cross. For Peter, his course on this earth ended with the cross. In the case of the Apostle Paul, he was forever applying the cross. Regardless of where the cross is located in our course, it is something we all must face. We must not try to sidestep the cross of Jesus, veer away from our personal cross or cast it aside because it is unpleasant. We must become identified with Jesus and His cross, embrace our personal cross, and be quick to apply it when we are being tested to betray what we know is true and right. We must allow the preconceived failure of the cross to signal our demise in order to become victorious souls in the kingdom of God.

-RJK

- The cross represents the Lord's battle to establish His kingly authority, whereas His heavenly life shows Him forth as triumphant and reigning.

-Watchmen Nee

- We cannot please God by what we do for Him in our own human effort, we can only please Him by surrendering and letting Him work in and through our lives.

-John Mulinde

- All I can say is I look for perpetual conflicts and struggles in this life, and I hope for no other peace, only a cross, while on this side of eternity."

-George Whitefield

But God forbid that I should glory, save in the cross of our Lord Jesus Christ, by whom the world is crucified unto me, and I unto the world (Galatians 6:14).

- This brings us to how we can and must overcome the influences of the flesh in our lives. It comes down to crucifying the flesh with all of its affections and lusts. To crucify the flesh means to nail it to a cross. We must force it to give way to its demise. It will not go gracefully. It will hide and play dead behind religion. It will act as if reformed to maintain its power. It will cry "foul" and mourn as if repentant. However, it is all show. The flesh can be nothing more than what it is: unclean and marked for judgment. It can do no less than it always has done, and that is to reign through its lusts.

-RJK

That no flesh should glory in his presence (1 Corinthians 1:29).

- You and I are nothing without the cross.

-Fenelon
(SH, pg. 25)

- All kings when they die have their power extinguished with their life: but Christ crucified is worshipped by the whole world. We proclaim The Crucified, and the devils tremble...

-Cyril of Jerusalem
(GPQ, pg. 68)

Thou believest that there is one God; thou doest well: The devils also believe, and tremble (James 2:19).

- To DIE TO SELF, or to come from under its power, IS NOT AND CAN NOT BE DONE by any active resistance we can make against it OR by our own power of nature. The one true way of dying to self is the way of patience, meekness, humility, surrender, and RESIGNATION to God.

-Andrew Murray

- Contrary to what might be expected, I look back on experience that at the time seemed especially desolating and painful with particular satisfaction. Indeed, I can say with complete truthfulness that everything I have learned in my seventy-five years in this world, everything that has truly enhanced and enlightened my experience, has been through affliction and not through happiness, whether pursued or attained. In other words, if it were ever possible to eliminate affliction from our earthly existence by means of some drug or other medical mumbo jumbo...the result would make it too banal and trivial to be endurable. This, of course is what the cross signifies. And it is the Cross that has called me inexorably to Christ.

-Malcolm Muggeridge

Then said Jesus unto his disciples, If any man will come after me, let him deny himself, and take up his cross, and follow me (Matthew 16:24).

- Our need for God will bring us to the foot of the cross, seeking Him as our source of life. It is here that we finally put all of our reliance on Him. When the great "I WILL" of arrogance has been brought down to the "I NEED" of humility, God is able to receive us.

  -RJK

- God prepares a cross for you that you must embrace without thought of self-preservation. The cross is painful, accept the cross and you will find peace even in the middle of turmoil.

  -Fenelon
  (SH, pg. 3)

- Our mission is not to lure believers out of existing groups. The road to restoring the Church is an inner way, the way of the cross, the way of shame and suffering. But it is also the way of unspeakable peace and refreshment unimagined by the world. This way is full of joy, glory, and happiness.

  -Manfred Haller
  (CA, pg. 153)

- When you consider salvation, it means deliverance. However, we are saved and delivered through death. We die to self to come into subjection to the Lordship of Jesus. We reckon ourselves dead to come into submission to God's plan, and we walk in death through obedience to His Word to discover the abundant life. This is the route Jesus traveled in His humanity, and it is the one we must travel to come to spiritual maturity or perfection. Clearly, it is by way of death to the self-life and the influences of the world that we come into perfection in our lives in Christ.

  -RJK

Knowing this, that our old man is crucified with him, that the body of sin might be destroyed, that henceforth we should not serve sin (Romans 6:6).

- Volunteer for your own death, for God will only accomplish His work to the extent you let Him.

-Fenelon
(SH, pg. 4)

- When Jesus told His disciples to daily pick up a personal cross and follow Him, it had nothing to do with sacrifice, but with being willing to experience whatever personal loss was necessary to gain life in Him.

-RJK

But what things were gain to me, those I counted loss for Christ (Philippians 3:7).

- It horribly skews the meaning of the cross when contemporary prophets of self-esteem say that the cross is a witness to my infinite worth...The biblical perspective is that the cross is a witness to the infinite worth of God's glory, and a witness to the immensity of the sin of my pride.

- John Piper

- You must live as if you were to die each day. Then you will be quite ready, for our preparation for death simply consists of detaching ourselves from the world to attach ourselves to God.

-Fenelon
(SH, pg. 53)

- Liberty in Christ has always been threatened by the vanity of this world, the temptation of the flesh, and the snares of Satan. The world has vain attractions, the flesh empty desires, and Satan the power to enslave his victims into the realm of nothingness and death. However, we have the glorious hope that we have indeed been delivered by the work of Christ on the cross.

-RJK

- Take courage! The work of God can only be done by the destruction of the self-life. May he sustain you, comfort you, make you poor, and help you experience the truth of that beautiful word, "Blessed are the poor in spirit."

-Fenelon
(TWG, pg. 87)

Blessed are the poor in spirit: for theirs is the kingdom of heaven (Matthew 5:3).

Revelation of Christ

❖ It is from the perspective of discovering God that we realize we must find Him in the midst of the confusing, pagan, idolatrous ways of self, the world, and Satan. He is the great treasure hidden by the darkness of the world, the garden that has yet to be discovered behind unseen walls of unbelief, the refreshing spring that must be uncapped, and the bread from heaven that must be gathered in faith, prepared in obedience, and partaken of to ensure life. He is in all that pertains to life and godliness, and must fill all to overflowing.

-RJK

❖ In order to believe truly in the Son, we must believe that He is the Son.

-Clement of Alexandria

He saith unto them, But whom say ye that I am? And Simon Peter answered and said, Thou art the Christ, the Son of the living God (Matthew 16:15-16).

❖ We must believe in Him, we must apprehend Him. We must worship Him, and it is these acts which must stand in place of our describing Him.

-Hilary of Poitiers
(GPQ, pg. 117)

❖ He might have withstood the plottings and devices of wicked men. Yes, He might have saved Himself. He had the power; but then He would never have been our Saviour! For no man can save himself who saves another.

-Peter Marshall
(JMM, pg. 94)

❖ He cannot be seen, for He is too bright for sight; nor can He be grasped, for He is too pure to touch; nor can He be measured, for He is too great for the senses.

-Mark Minucius Felix
(GPQ, pg. 117)

❖ In the light of His origin and character it is impossible to believe that he did not rise from the dead. With His Resurrection everything else that has been revealed of Him assumes proportion, order and harmony; without it all is a mystery; a lock without a key; a labyrinth without a clue; a beginning without a corresponding end.

-Dr. Graham Scroggie

❖ From a knowledge of His work, we shall know Him.

-Robert Boyle

❖ As the tabernacle in our midst, Jesus would reveal that holiness is a state from within. As the High Priest, He showed the measure of service that is acceptable. As the sacrifice, His blood would purge the heirs of salvation from all unrighteousness and serve as the means to remit their sins by producing the means of forgiveness and reconciliation.

-RJK

❖ Deny His deity, and you have no answer to His perfect sincerity, unselfishness, and humility.

-Herbert Lockyer

Who did no sin, neither was guile found in his mouth (1 Peter 2:22).

❖ I preached with some life and spirituality, and was enabled to speak closely against selfish religion that loves Christ for His benefits, but not for Himself.

-David Brainerd
(LDD, pg.116)

******

The Witness of His Work

Intellectually and morally, Christ is Christianity. Detach Christianity from Christ and it vanishes before your eyes into intellectual vapor. For it is of the essence of Christianity that, day by day, hour by hour, the Christian should live in conscious, felt, sustained relationship to the ever-living Author of his creed and life. Christianity is non-existent apart from Christ; it centres in Christ; it radiates, now as at the first, from Christ. He is indissolubly associated with every movement of the Christian's deepest life. "I live," exclaims the Apostle, "yet not I, 'but Christ liveth in me'." When we do see the Bridegroom's face,

We will not gaze at glory,
  But on our King of Grace:
Not at the crown He giveth,
  But on His pierced hand;
The Lamb is all the glory
  Of Immanuel's land.

-Canon Little
(MP, pg. 166)

❖ The holy vocation of Jesus took Him to the cross, and His resurrection was God's receipt for Calvary, the seal that the debt has been paid. Such a triumph over Satan, and over his power of death, earned for Jesus immortal honor and worship.

-Hebert Lockyer
(MP, pg. 161)

❖ Let nothing glitter in your eyes apart from Him.

-Ignatius
(GPQ, pg. 46)

- The Christian faith is, thus not merely one religion among many. It is the true revelation of the one true God of creation, the record of His provision of forgiveness and salvation. All human religions betray their humanistic origin by their humanly attainable standards, whereas God's way of salvation is by His grace, received only by faith. "Not by works of righteousness which we have done, but according to his mercy he saved us."

  -Henry Morris

Not by works of righteousness which we have done, but according to his mercy he saved us, by the washing of regeneration, and renewing of the Holy Ghost (Titus 3:5).

- Our ascended Lord gives hope for two ages. In the age to come, He is the judge, rejecting unrighteousness, isolating His enemies to hell, blessing His new creation in Christ. In this age, His Holy Spirit is with us, calling nations to follow Christ's path, uniting people through Christ's love.

  -Hymnal

- He became man; He did not merely enter into a man.

  -Athanasius
  (GPQ. Pg. 148)

- Hating sin, He yet bore it. Although He made Himself responsible for it, He was never defiled by it. He was not able to save Himself from the sufferings of the cross. He could not because He would not.

  -Herbert Lockyer
  (MP, pg. 135)

******

Who Killed Jesus?

Through the years people have debated about who killed Jesus. Sadly, the Jews have been the scapegoat for centuries. Practically every tyrant and despot has pointed a finger at the Jews and accused them as being the instigators behind every ailment of society including the murder of Jesus. They have suffered unimaginable atrocities, sometimes in the name of Christ. Granted, the religious Jewish leadership planned, insisted, and stirred up the crowd to demand Jesus' crucifixion. However, they could have not crucified Him without the Roman leader, Pilate's permission.

Pilate was the one who possessed the authority to determine who would live or die. This fact is brought out in John 18:31 and 19:10. We also know the Roman soldiers would have to carry out the execution. In a sick attempt to save Jesus' life, we can see where Pilate offered Jesus to be beaten to serve as a sort of "peace offering" with the Jews to silence their demands for His death. However, it did not suffice them. Pilate's unwillingness to reject their demands allowed Jesus to be crucified. Herod also had the power to stop it, but hid behind the technicality that had to do with jurisdiction, while allowing Him to be mocked by his soldiers because the Lord would not entertain him by doing a miracle.

As we can see, the Jews were not the only ones who were involved in the crucifixion of Jesus. The Roman leaders held the authority, but remained indecisive and indifferent. Who killed Jesus? The Lord answered that question, "No one!" In John 10:18, He made it clear that no man could take His life. He would lay it down in order to obey His Father's will and plan in regard to redemption. He had come to give His life and would ensure the fulfillment of it under His own volition. Jesus came to serve as God's sacrificial Lamb. He was the One who gave up His life on our behalf, knowing that He possessed the power as deity to once again take it back.

Therefore doth my Father love me, because I lay down my life, that I might take it again. No man taketh it from me, but I lay it down of myself, I have power to lay it down, and I have power to take it again. This commandment have I received of my Father (John 10:17-18).

❖ The Son of God became a man to enable men to become the sons of God.

-C. S. Lewis
(HFG, pg. 167)

- In glory He is incomprehensible, in greatness unfathomable, in height inconceivable, in power incomparable, in wisdom unrivalled, in goodness inimitable, in kindness unutterable.

  -Theophilus of Antioch
  (GPQ. pg. 117)

- The puritan, Thomas Watson, talked about how we could not look into the Godhead without Jesus first clothing Himself in humanity. Because of Christ we now can delight in the revelation that was unveiled in Christ. Watson went on to explain how it was a custom of old among shepherds to clothe themselves with sheepskins, to become acceptable to the sheep. He then goes on to make this statement, "So Christ clothed Himself with our flesh, that the divine nature may be more pleasing to us. . . .Through the lantern of Christ's humanity we may behold the light of the light of the Deity. (PDC, pg. 374)

For in him dwelleth all the fullness of the Godhead bodily (Colossians 2:9).

- "I know men, and I tell you that Jesus is not a man. The religion of Christ is a mystery which subsists by its own force, and proceeds from a mind which is not a human mind. We find in it a marked individuality, which originated a train of words and actions unknown before. Jesus is not a philosopher, for His proofs are miracles, and from the first His disciples adored Him. Alexander, Caesar, Charlemagne, and myself founded empires; but on what foundation did we rest the creatures of our genius? Upon force. But Jesus Christ founded an empire upon love; and at this hour millions of men would die for Him. I die before my time, and my body will be given back to the earth to become food for worms. Such is the fate of him who has been called the great Napoleon. What an abyss between my deep misery and the eternal kingdom of Christ, which is proclaimed, loved, adored, and is still existing over the whole earth!" Then, turning to General Bertrand, the emperor added, "If you do not perceive that Jesus Christ is God, I did wrong in appointing you a general."

-Napoleon Bonaparte

- Jesus is the One who uncaps the Living Water of the Spirit in the soul. This is why He sent forth the invitation to come to Him. The reality is that there is so much in the soul of man that would hinder the flow of these rivers. There are walls of fear and the boulders of wounds and unforgiveness that block the way. There are barren wildernesses of unbelief that will absorb such water without it making any real impact on people's lives.

-RJK

But whosoever drinketh of the water that I shall give him shall never thirst; but the water that I shall give him shall be in him a well of water springing up into everlasting life (John 4:14).

******

No Distant Lord

No distant Lord have I,
    Loving afar to be,
Made flesh for me He cannot rest
    Until He rests in me.

I need not journey far
    This dearest friend to see,
Companionship is always mine,
    He makes His home with me.

I envy not the twelve,
    Nearer to me is He,
The life He once lived here on earth
    He lives again in me.

Ascended now to God
My witness there to be,
His witness here am I because
His Spirit dwells in me.

O glorious Son of God,
Incarnate Deity,
I shall forever be with Thee
Because Thou art with me.

-Maltbie D. Babcock
(HFG, pg, 241)

❖ A dark hour makes Jesus bright.

-Robert Murray McCheyne

Who being the brightness of his glory, and the express image of his person, and upholding all things by the word of his power, when he had by himself purged our sins, sat down on the right hand of the Majesty on high (Hebrews 1:3).

❖ Oswald Chambers talked about the wonder of the Incarnation. Jesus slipped into ordinary childhood. His transfiguration caused such awe, but He had to descend into the demon-possessed valleys, which eventually led Him to the cross and into a grave. However, His journey did not end in a grave, He emerged in resurrection power. It is with this in mind that Chambers points out that Christians often look for the marvelous. Yet, there is so much of the ordinary that envelopes us that it is hard to go through each day glorifying our Lord. The ordinary can cause us to look for heroes. Chambers goes on to say, "It is one thing to go through a crisis grandly, but a different thing to go through every day glorifying God when there is no witness, no limelight, and no one paying the remotest attention to you. If we don't want medieval haloes, we want something that will make people say—What a wonderful man of prayer he is! What a pious, devoted woman she is! If anyone says that of you, you have not been loyal to God."

❖ We know that the death of Christ was the death of the cross. We know that that death of the cross is His Chief glory. Without the death, He would not be the Christ.

-Andrew Murray

For he hath made him to be sin for us, who knew no sin; that we might be made the righteousness of God in him (2 Corinthians 5:21).

❖ Do not look at your sin--it will discourage you!
Do not look at your self--it will distress you!
Do not look at Satan--he will bewilder you!
Do not look to men--they will deceive, or disappoint you!
Do not look at your trials--they will deject you!
"Let us throw off everything that hinders and the sin that so easily entangles, and let us run with perseverance the race marked out for us--looking unto Jesus, the author and perfecter of our faith!" Hebrews 12:1-2
Look only, look always, look intently--to Jesus!
Run looking, work looking, fight looking, suffer looking, live looking, and die looking--to Jesus, who is at God's right hand in glory.
Oh, look, look, look to Jesus!

-James Smith

❖ We change, He changes not;
Our Christ can never die.
His love, not ours, the resting place,
His truth, not mine, the tie.

-James Elliot
(SOA, pg.158)

❖ John Owens related how it is easy to love, delight, serve, believe, obey, and put our trust in God because of the revelation of Christ. He made this statement, "Likewise, the difference between believers and unbelievers is not so much in the *matter* of their knowledge of God as in the *manner* of their knowledge. The excellency of a believer does not consist in how much he knows, but in what he assimilates and what becomes transformed within his soul." (ST, pg. 184)

❖ The most important part of our task will be to tell everyone who will listen that Jesus is the only answer to the problems that are disturbing the hearts of men and nations. We shall have the right to speak because we can tell from our experience that His light is more powerful than the deepest darkness...How wonderful that the reality of His presence is greater than the reality of the hell around us.

-Betsie ten Boom, to her sister, Corrie
Concentration Camp
(HFG, pg. 59)

❖ Do not let anything catch your eye beside Him, for whom I carry around these chains—my spiritual pearls!

-Ignatius
(GPQ, pg. 16)

❖ Prayer enthrones God as sovereign and elevates Jesus Christ to sit with Him.

-E. M. Bounds
(WOP, pg. 109)

❖ Did travailing pains come in with sins? We read of the travail of Christ's soul. Did subjection come in with sin? Christ was made under the law. Did the curse come in with sin? Christ was made a curse for us, died a cursed death. Did thorns come in with sin? He was crowned with thorns for us. Did sweat come in with sin? He for us did sweat as it were great drops of blood. Did sorrow come in with sin? He was a man of sorrows. Did death come in with sin? He became obedient unto death. Thus is the plaster as wide as the wound. Blessed be God for Jesus Christ!

-Matthew Henry

Christ hath redeemed us from the curse of the law, being made a curse for us; for it is written, Cursed is every one that hangeth on a tree (Galatians 3:13).

❖ What those who chided Him were ignorant of was the wonderful truth that because He was the Son the Father delighted in, He stayed upon the cross till the bitter end in order to complete God's redemptive plan. Jesus could not save Himself and us at the same time. Salvation became ours through His sacrifice.

-Herbert Lockyer
(MP, pg. 151)

❖ The resurrected Christ embodies a totally new creation.

-Manfred Haller
(CA, pg. 7)

❖ Jesus Christ must graduate from the romantic position of Savior and become Lord of our lives. He must cease from being a mere prophet and become the Son of God. He must be allowed to leave the manger as a baby and become the Lamb of God who died on the cross as our personal substitute. He must not just be sentimentally adored as a sacrifice on the cross; He must be recognized and worshipped as the One who has risen from the grave and now sits on the right hand of the Father. He must not remain just an expression of God's love, but He must become the motivating reason for doing what is right and coming to a place of holiness before God. As the Apostle Paul pointed out, Jesus must become our all in all.

-RJK

❖ No one can be one with Christ who is not Christlike.

-Hannah Whitall Smith
(CHL, pg. 227)

For whom he did foreknow, he also did predestinate to be conformed to the image of his Son, that he might be the firstborn among many brethren (Romans 8:29).

❖ How could Christ have died for sinners if He Himself were in sin?

-John Chrysostom

- Love is the highest glory of God. But this love was a hidden mystery until it was manifest in Christ Jesus.

  -Andrew Murray

- To please Jesus--becomes his delight.
  To be like Jesus--becomes his highest desire.
  To be with Jesus--becomes his Heaven.

  -James Smith

******

Christ-Centered?

In his book, *God's Goal: Christ as All in All,* Manfred Haller explains how the modern-day Church is missing God's real goal. The Church is missing God's real purpose because the matters of heaven often become about man, rather than man realizing what he has in Christ. By directing all spiritual matters towards man, instead of directing man towards the essence of all spiritual matters, Jesus Christ, the Church has become man-centered rather than Christ-centered.

The Bible speaks of the necessity of Christ being in all matters and becoming the complete sum in all that is being done and will be accomplished in His kingdom. God's goal is to get us to realize that Christ is all in all. In other words, it is not just a matter of Jesus dying for us, but that His Spirit and life lives in us. His act of sacrifice on the cross was not just a matter of God loving us, but that since He is the essence of love, He could do nothing but pay the necessary price. Salvation begins with the work of Christ, is brought forth in accordance to the truth about Christ, and will come to fruition when the fullness of His life is realized in us.

Clearly, it all comes down to the emphasis. So much emphasis is being put on what Jesus did on behalf of man. Notice that such a presentation ends with man. However, if we begin with Jesus' sacrificial act, and explain it in relationship to who He is and why He did it, we end with the revelation of Him in His glory. Coming back to center in a matter entails more than just starting from the right premise, it must also end with the right focus.

Haller made this statement in his book, "Today's Christology is not an authentic Christology at all. It ends up being just a loosely applied soteriology (from the Greek word "soter," meaning savior). It is one-sided and top-heavy. Upon closer scrutiny, we see that traditional Christology has rather little to do with the Person revealed in the New Testament. Many denominations call their teaching Christ-centered, but the Son, His person, and His place in the holy counsel of God is not their centerpoint."

He goes on to explain that God's purpose is to replace everything about us as a means to place Christ in us. After all, Christ is everything, and our entire salvation is contained in the fact that we have received Him. Haller reiterates this point by saying, "Churches do not need more love; they need more of Christ, for Christ is love. We do not need more patience; Christ is the patience in us. We do not need more power per se, but Christ; for Christ is the power in us. It is not that Jesus dispenses whatever qualities or gifts we need at any particular time. Rather, it is the fact that Christ in you is the fullness of what you require. This Jesus, who is in you, is limitless and inexhaustible."

He that descended is the same also that ascended up far above all heavens, that he might fill all things (Ephesians 4:10).

❖ People transpose their own ideas of what they would do if they were all-powerful onto God. They forget God's power is just one aspect of His character. He is so much more, and all of His attributes contribute to His intervention in people's lives. Therefore, His intervention is not based on His ability to do great things, but on His great character to work the impossible in a situation that will cause spiritual growth for His followers and bring Him glory.

-RJK

****

He Has Done All Things Well

Yes, from first to last, from our cradle to our grave, from the earliest pang of sin's conviction, to the last thrill of sin's forgiveness, from earth to heaven--this will be our testimony in all the way the Lord our God has led us in the wilderness: "He has done all things well!"

In providence and in grace,
in every truth of His Word,
in every lesson of His love,
in every stroke of His rod,
in every sunbeam that has shone,
in every cloud that has shaded,
in every element that has sweetened,
in every ingredient that has embittered,
in all that has been mysterious, inscrutable, painful, and humiliating,
in all that He gave,
in all that He took away,
this testimony is His just due, and this our grateful acknowledgment through time and through eternity: "He has done all things well!"

-Octavius Winslow

And were beyond measure astonished, saying, He hath done all things well: he maketh both the deaf to hear, and the dumb to speak. (Mark 7:37)

- God does not do things to prove he is God; rather, He does them because He is God.

  -RJK

- Job is a lesson in acceptance, not blind resignation but of believing acceptance, that what God does is well done.

  -James Elliot
  (SOA, pg. 184)

The Truth About God's Word

- Show me a person who despises Bible reading, or thinks little of Bible preaching, and I hold it to be a certain fact that they are not yet born again. They may be zealous about forms and ceremonies. They may be diligent in attending church and the taking of the Lord's Supper. But if these things are more precious to them than the Bible, I cannot believe that they are converted. Tell me what the Bible is to a person and I will generally tell you what they are. This is the pulse to try—this is the barometer to look at—if we would know the state of the heart. I have no notion of the Spirit dwelling in a person and not giving clear evidence of His presence. And I believe it to be clear evidence of the Spirit's presence when the Word is really precious to a person's soul.

  -J. C. Ryle

- It is better to dwell alone with the Lord than to sit in the house of error.

  -Jeannette Haley

- If you believe you cannot be deceived, you are already deceived.

  -RJK

- I would not, for a chapel full of gold, recede from the truth.

  -John (Jan) Huss
  (Just before he was martyred)

- The heart of Christianity is the Bible, God's infallible Word; the heart of the Bible is the cross of the Redeemer; the heart of the cross is the very heart of God, making provision for the salvation of a lost world.

-Herbert Lockyer
(MP, pg. 146)

- The true spirit of Bible study is a readiness to believe every promise implicitly and to obey every command unhesitatingly.

-Andrew Murray

- Simple and undisguised truth is the most clear for it has sufficient ornament of itself. For this reason, it is corrupted when it is embellished with external ornamentation.

-Lactantius
(DCB, pg. 549)

- Apostasy is a very interesting word. It means to fall away from the center as to what is true, pure, and right. The truth is every aspect of society is basically going apostate. The home is falling away from moral accountability, leaving the family unprotected. Society is falling away from godly principles, leaving it open for complete failure and ruin. Religion is falling away from immovable truths, opening it up for indifference, fanaticism, and judgment.

-RJK

- What is needed is not the authority of the one who argues, but the truth of the argument itself.

-Mark Minucius Felix

- It is out of truth that falsehood is built; out of religion that superstition is compacted.

-Tertullian
(GPQ, pg. 130)

- If a book be false in its facts, disprove them; if false in it reasoning, refute it. But for God's sake, let us freely hear both sides if we choose.

-Thomas Jefferson

For we can do nothing against the truth, but for the truth (2 Corinthians 13:8).

- Many people are faithful to their own beliefs, but not to the truth. The only way we will be faithful to the truth is we must learn to love it.

  -RJK

And with all deceivableness of unrighteousness in them that perish; because they received not the love of the truth that they might be saved (2 Thessalonians 2:10).

- Defend the Bible? I would just as soon defend a lion. Just turn the Bible loose. It will defend itself.

  - Charles Spurgeon

- I perceived how that it was impossible to establish the lay people in any truth except the Scripture were plainly laid before their eyes in their mother tongue.

  -William Tyndale

- The Bible, the true Word of God, gives the only account of the creation of the universe, then reports the only resurrection from the dead, and finally uniquely reveals God's grace in providing salvation by faith apart from works, recognizing the impossibility of attaining God's perfect standard by human effort. The Lord Jesus Christ, our Creator and Redeemer, gives eternal life to all who trust their souls to Him.

  -Henry Morris

- Truth that is never applied to everyday living, simply remains an intellectual notion that has no life or power to it.

  -RJK

- Read whatever doctrine of Scripture you will and it will leave you as poor and empty and unreformed as it found you, unless it has turned you wholly and solely to the Spirit of God.

  -William Law
  (WRP, pg.8)

- Ignorance of scripture is the mother of error, not devotion... The Scripture contains in it the *credenda*, the things which we are to believe, and the *agenda,* the things which we are to practice.

  -Thomas Watson
  Puritan Minister
  (PDC, pg. 216)

Thy word is true from the beginning: and every one of thy righteous judgments endureth forever (Psalm 119:160).

- The power of truth is so great that it defends itself by its own clarity.

  -Lactantius
  (DCB, pg. 549)

- As at least on-half of all the Old Testament forecasts converge upon the Lord Jesus Christ, such predictive prophecy is not only an impregnable rock fortress for rational faith, defying all attempted assaults, but a double defense, proving the divine origin, inspiration, and authority of Scripture—and a vindication of His deity and messiahship.

  -Herbert Lockyer
  (MP, pg. 147)

Knowing this first, that no prophecy of the scripture is of any private interpretation. For the prophecy came not in old time by the will of man: but holy men of God spake as they were moved by the Holy Ghost (2 Peter 1:20-21).

- The Bible is either absolute, or it's obsolete.

  Leonard Ravenhill

- When we have comprehended spiritual truths purely by means of the intellect, they are only a knowledge of reality. They are only concepts until they take hold of us, have power over us. Only then have we encountered them as reality.

-Manfred Haller

******

A Lamp for My Feet

God's Word is represented as a lamp for the feet. It is a "lamp"--not a blazing sun, nor even a lighthouse--but a plain, common lamp or lantern which one can carry about in the hand.

It is a lamp "for the feet," not throwing its beams afar, not illumining a hemisphere--but shining only on the one little bit of road on which the pilgrim's feet are walking.

The law of divine guidance is, "Step by step."

-J. R. Miller

Thy word is a lamp unto my feet, and a light unto my path (Psalm 119:105).

- He who wrests the words of the Lord according to his own pleasure, and saith there is no resurrection and judgment, is the first-born of Satan.

-Polycarp
(GPQ, pg. 32)

- Sound doctrine does not enter into a hard and disobedient heart.

-Justin Martyr
(DCB, pg. 547)

- People do not believe lies because they have to, but because they want to.

-Malcolm Muggeridge

❖ When sin affects our mind by deceitfulness we lose the life, power, sense, and impression of the Word.

-John Owen
(ST, pg. 51)

❖ Don't try to bring the Word of God down to your level. Let it pull you up to its level.

-David MacDonald

The way of man is forward and strange: but as for the pure, his work is right (Proverbs 21:8).

❖ If their age does not prove the Scriptures divine, then their majesty does.

-Tertullian
(GPQ, pg. 29)

******

The Bible

The Holy Bible is a perfect Book from our perfect God. It is His love letter to us. Here the Father plans, the Son executes, the Spirit operates. The way of salvation is given; Heaven is revealed; Hell is described. The cross is its center, eternal life its fruition, and God's glory its end. By it the soul is cultured, the mind enlightened, the memory enriched, and the heart established.

The Bible is the traveler's guide, the pilgrim's staff, the warrior's sword, and the fighter's shield. It is the telescope of faith, the microscope of conscience, the mirror of Christ's face, and the casket (or jewel box) of God's grace. It is food for the heart-hungry, drink for the soul-thirsty, medicine for the sin-sick, and life for the spiritually dead.

Read it to be godly; use it to be fruitful; believe it to be faithful; trust it to have peace. God has magnified His Word above His great name, and has commanded that it be preached and practiced. It is His standard of judgment. By it all are wooed and waned, saved or doomed. Read it in the company of the Author. Be a Bible-read, Bible-fed Christian. It covers the course of time between two eternities and will live forever.

-Author Unknown

- The Bible definitely is infallible, how else could it survive so many years of bad preaching?

- Leonard Ravenhill

All scripture is given by inspiration of God, and is profitable for doctrine, for reproof, for correction, for instruction in righteousness (2 Timothy 3:16).

******

Touching the Wings of God

It has always been interesting to me to discover how the Jewish people weaved into their clothing and rituals points of remembrance. They were told to remember the Law as a means to remember not only their God, but who they were to be as far as His people. They had the phylacteries, the Passover, and the prayer shawl to mention a few reminders that pointed to and reminded them of the seriousness to keep God's Word ever before them.

It is interesting to also see how the Jewish people broke down the Law as a means to remember them. For example, there were 613 laws established in the Law of Moses (the Torah). In Ruth Specter Lascelle's book, *Jewish Faith and the New Covenant,* she revealed how for generations the orthodox dogmas of Judaism was that there were 248 positive commandments, which would be in correspondence of the 248 body parts, and there were 365 negative commandments that correlated with 365 sinews of the body. Clearly the positive aspect of the Law kept matters functioning, but the negative parts of the Law held everything in place.

The other interesting way in which the Jewish people remembered the Law was the prayer shawl. According to Numbers 15:39 they were to look at the prayer shawl and remember His commandments. The main part of the article that pointed to the Law were the fringes that hung from the borders of the prayer shawl. They were also referred to as wings. The Hebrew word for "fringes" is Tsitzith. Tsitzith in the gematria (numerology) equals 600. When you take the eight strands that make up these fringes and add the five knots that were to be tied into each set of eight fringes, you have 613, the number of the laws found in the Torah.

When the woman with the issue of blood grabbed Jesus' shawl, she actually grabbed the fringes or wings of it. No doubt she understood the implication of grabbing hold of the wings of the Lord's garment. She knew there was healing in the wings established by God. She was not disappointed in clinging to the symbol of the Written Law, for in the end she received healing from the Living Word. How we need to cling to Scripture by faith in order to receive life and healing from the Living Word of heaven.

But unto you that fear my name shall the Sun of righteousness arise with healing in his wings; and ye shall go forth, and grow up like calves of the stall (Malachi 4:2). Emphasis added.

❖ Seek and find, and realize that the truth does not lie openly on the surface.

-Clement
(GPQ, pg. 182)

❖ Truth mixed with error is equivalent to all error, except that it is more innocent looking and, therefore, more dangerous. God hates such a mixture! Any error, or any truth-and-error mixture, calls for definite exposure and repudiation. To condone such is to be unfaithful to God and His Word and treacherous to imperiled souls for whom Christ died.

-H. A. Ironside

Your glorying is not good. Know ye not that a little leaven leaveneth the whole lump (1 Corinthians 5:6).

❖ Truth between candid minds can never do harm.

-Thomas Jefferson

- ❖ Again I say, there is all the difference in the world between knowing the Word of God and knowing the God of the Word.

-Leonard Ravenhill

- ❖ Truth is like a vast cavern into which we desire to enter, but we are not able to traverse alone.

-Charles Spurgeon
(FCB, pg. 288)

But the Comforter, who is the Holy Ghost, whom the Father will send in my name, he shall teach you all things, and bring all things to your remembrance, whatever I have said unto you (John 14:26).

- ❖ The Scriptures come first. If you are in doubt upon any subject, you must, first of all, consult the Bible about it, and see whether there is any law to direct you. Until you have found and obeyed God's will as it is there revealed, you must not ask nor expect a separate, direct, personal revelation. A great many fatal mistakes are made in the matter of guidance by the overlooking of this simple rule.

-Hannah Whitall Smith

- ❖ The joy and the blessing of God's Word is only to be known by doing it.

-Andrew Murray

******

Each time I looked at the Word of God, His truth,

my busyness stopped.

The fragments of my life became still,

And I knew without a doubt

His peace that passeth all understanding.

A sense of direction came for my life.

A pattern emerged for me to follow—

like a weaving of a tapestry—

when finished, a life in Christ will show.

May He perfect that which is weak in me!

-Maureen Human

- God's Word is the only authentic revelation of God's will.

  -Andrew Murray

If any man will do his will, he shall know of the doctrine, whether it be of God, or whether I speak of myself (John 7:17).

- "But they were written by unlearned and ignorant men, and should not therefore be readily believed." See that this be not rather a stronger reason for believing that they have not been adultered by any false statements, but were put forth by men of simple mind, who knew not how to trick out their tales with meretricious ornaments.

  -Arnobius
  (GPQ, pg. 30)

- It seems many Christians would rather put on their spiritual diapers of foolish expectation and suck on the pacifier of untested doctrine by standing on feelings and emotions instead of putting on their armor and standing on both the Rock (Jesus Christ) and the Word of God.

  -RJK

- Truth wears well. Time tests it, but it right well endures the trial.

  -Charles Spurgeon
  (FCB, pg. 65)

- George Mueller said that he learned not to stop reading the Word until he felt happy in God. Then he felt prepared to go out and do His work.

❖ Ignorance of the Scripture is ignorance of Christ.

-Jerome
(GPQ, pg. 33)

❖ The letter of Scripture brings death when it is built into systems of strife and contention about words, ideas, and opinions, and when it causes the kingdom of God to consist of mere words rather than of power.

-William Law
(WRP, pg. 95)

For the kingdom of God is not in word, but in power (1 Corinthians 4:20).

❖ Oh, give yourself up with an undivided heart to learn in the Scriptures what God says and seeks of you.

-Andrew Murray

❖ Everything else will fail, but His Word never will.

Charles Spurgeon

But the word of the Lord endureth forever. And this is the word which by the gospel is preached unto you (1 Peter 1:25).

❖ The battle that rages today is not for the head, but for the heart. It is not the head of man that must be enlightened. It is the heart that must be circumcised by the sword of God's Word before it can rightly perceive and embrace truth, thereby, enlarging man's ability to properly understand and receive spiritual matters.

-RJK

❖ I do not accept what you introduce apart from Scripture.

-Tertullian
(GPQ, pg. 31)

******

Preach the Word
Charles Wesley

Shall I, for fear of mortal man,
The Spirit's course in me restrain?
Or, undismayed, in deed and word
Be a true witness to my Lord

Awed by a mortal's frown, shall I
Conceal the Word of God most high?
How then before Thee shall I dare
To stand, or how Thine anger bear

Shall I, to sooth the unholy throng
Soften Thy truths, and smooth my tongue?
To gain earth's guilded toys, or flee
The Cross, endured my Lord, by Thee.

What then is he whose scorn I dread.
Whose wrath or hate makes me afraid?
A man! An heir of death, a slave
To sin! A bubble on the wave!

Yea! Let men rage, since Thou wilt spread
Thy shadowing wings about my head;
Since in all pain Thy tender love
Will still my sure refreshment prove.

Give me Thy strength, O God of power;
Then let winds blow or tempests roar;
Thy faithful witness will I be;
"Tis fixed; I can do all through Thee.

(TB, pg. 258)

The Character and Work of the Holy Spirit

- Mortification is only accomplished through the Spirit...Mortification based on human strength, carried out with man-made schemes, always ends in self-righteousness. This is the essence and substance of all false religion in the world.

  -John Owen

- We must be careful not to choose, but to let God's Holy Spirit manage our lives; not to smooth down and explain away, but to stir up the gift and allow God's Spirit to disturb us and disturb us and disturb us until we yield and yield and yield, and the possibility in God's mind for us becomes an established fact in our lives, with the rivers in evidence meeting the need of a dying world."

  -Smith Wigglesworth.

- In Acts 8, Philip was instructed to go to Gaza. Talk about going without understanding why! This is the reality of being led by the Spirit. It is a faith walk of obedience. Such a walk means being open for the unusual and available to that which is unexpected.

  -RJK

- You may ask, “why do we need teachers when the Bible says in 1 John 2:27 that we need no man to teach us if we have the Holy Ghost?” You need to understand that God gifts people, *through the Holy Spirit*, to teach His Word; but it is only *by* the Holy Spirit that God’s Word becomes *living* because of the anointing (of the Holy Spirit). In other words, teachers break the bread of the Word of life to our minds, but it is by the *quickening* of the Holy Spirit that this bread becomes *living* in our *hearts*!

-Jeannette Haley

- ❖ We need the intellect to hear and understand God's Word in its human meaning. But we need to know that the possession of the truth by intellect can only benefit us when the Holy Spirit makes it life and truth in the heart.

-Andrew Murray

But the anointing which ye have received of him abideth in you, and ye need not that any man teach you: but as the same anointing teacheth you of all things, and is truth, and is no lie, and even as it hath taught you, ye shall abide in him (1 John 2:27).

- ❖ Human nature never really changes unless it is regenerated by the Spirit of God. People want proof for that which is not tangible. Dr. G. A. Buttrick commented,

  Philip looks before he leaps;
  Peter leaps before he looks.
  Thomas was a dogged unbeliever until the last minute.
  Judas sought regeneration through revolution, instead of revolution through regeneration.
  James and John wanted to get rid of people who differed with them, instead of getting rid of the differences, so that they could get the people. (JMM, pg. 42)

- ❖ Pentecost is the breathtaking fact that in Christ the living God Himself came to reside in man through His Spirit. Pentecost is the indwelling of God, the Shekinah glory, in man—the birth of a new creation, a new humanity, the unveiling of new reality. What reality? Namely, "Christ in you, the hope of glory."

-Manfred Haller
(CA, pg. 8)

To whom God would make known what is the riches of the glory of this mystery among the Gentiles; which is Christ in you, the hope of glory (Colossians 1:27).

- We must sanctify our lives to God to ensure the cleansing of the terrain of our inner man that had been greatly affected by the imprint of sin upon our souls. The seal of the Holy Spirit in our lives must change that imprint. We must submit to the Spirit to ensure the lay of the land of our souls belong to the Lord. It is His Spirit that identifies us as our Lord's possession, and it is the life of our Lord in us that distinguishes us as the servant of the Most High.

  -RJK

- The world is not waiting for a new definition of the Holy Ghost but a new demonstration of the Holy Ghost.

  -Leonard Ravenhill

And my speech and my preaching was not with enticing words of man's wisdom, but in demonstration of the Spirit and of power (1 Corinthians 2:4).

- Like a candle in the darkness, the Holy Spirit illuminates the deep recesses of the heart, exposing the subtle and deceitful schemes and imaginations of sin. Thus, the power of prayer penetrates sin and destroys it.

  -John Owen
  (ST, pg. 46)

- Revival cannot be organized, but we can set our sails to catch the wind from heaven when God chooses to blow upon His people once again.

  -G. Campbell Morgan

The wind bloweth where it listeth, and thou hearest the sound thereof, but canst not tell from whence it cometh, and whither it goeth: so is every one that is born of the Spirit (John 3:8).

- To live then, is Christ; and to understand is the Spirit.

  -Marcus Victorinus
  (GPQ, pg. 138)

- Elisha had more of the Holy Spirit, dead, than most Christians have of Him, alive.

  -Steve Wilburn

- Receiving the truth will bring changes to a person's life, but if people do not allow the Holy Spirit to convict of sin, then they quench the Spirit. If people do not allow Him to convict them of righteousness, then they grieve the Spirit. And, if they do not allow Him to convict them of impending judgment, then they can end up blaspheming the Spirit.

  -Jeannette Haley

- In studying the character of the Holy Spirit, we know that He is a gentleman. He will not move where He is not wanted. He will not pry where there is no desire for holiness or truth. In fact, He will be grieved over sin, quenched when there is a wrong spirit, vexed when there is no respect for righteousness, and absent when there is no holiness.

  -RJK

And the LORD said, My Spirit shall not always strive with man, for that he also is flesh: yet his days shall be an hundred and twenty years (Genesis 6:3).

- May the Spirit of Elijah, beloved reader, be upon us. If we seek it, we will have it. Oh, may the God of Elijah answer by fire, consume the spirit of worldliness in the churches, burn up the dross, and make us wholehearted Christians. May that Spirit come upon us; let that be our prayer upon our family altars and in our prayer closets. Let us cry mightily to God that we may have a double portion of the Holy Spirit and that we may not rest satisfied with this worldly state of living. Let us, like Samson, shake ourselves and come out from the world, that we may have the power of God.

-D.L. Moody

- Know thou that every man is either empty or full. For if he has not the Holy Spirit, he has no knowledge of the creator; he has not received Jesus Christ the life.

-Irenaeus
(GPQ, pg. 138)

- The building of our spiritual lives is not a matter of technically getting Scripture right, but one of Jesus being unveiled in Scripture by the Holy Spirit.

-RJK

- The Holy Spirit fills men—not "temples made with hands." All the stained-glass windows in the world, plus robed choirs and deep-throated organs, will not win the Holy Spirit to brood in a place brilliant and exotic to aesthetic taste. The Spirit dwells in a humble and contrite heart.

-Leonard Ravenhill

The LORD is nigh unto those who are of a broken heart; and saveth such as be of a contrite spirit (Psalm 34:18).

- The spirit that motivates us is like the rudder of a ship. It will determine which direction we will walk in our lives. If the spirit is of the natural man, it will be self-serving in its ways. If it is the spirit of the world, it will prove to be rebellious and unteachable. If it is the Spirit of God, He will always lead us to a greater revelation of Jesus.

-RJK

Howbeit when he, the Spirit of truth, is come, he will guide you into all truth: for he shall not speak of himself, but whatever he shall hear, that shall he speak; and he will show you things to come (John 16:13).

- If revival is being withheld from us it is because some idol remains still enthroned; because we still insist in placing our reliance in human schemes; because we still refuse to face the unchangeable truth that, 'It is not by might, but by My Spirit.

  -Jonathan Goforth

- We are told to walk after the Spirit as a means to fulfill righteousness. We are to be led by the Spirit to fulfill our destiny in regard to discovering our lives in Christ. But now we must begin to walk in the Spirit to be assured of not fulfilling the lust of the flesh. When you consider the reality of our life in Christ, you can see how complete it is. Walking after something disciplines the focus. Being led by something disciplines the walk. Walking in something disciplines the attitude. After all, walking in something shows us the source of that which is influencing us the most.

  -RJK

This I say then, Walk in the Spirit, and ye shall not fulfil the lust of the flesh (Galatians 5:16).

- (He makes) His ministers a flame of fire. Am I ignitable? God deliver me from the dread asbestos of "other things." Saturate me with the oil of the Spirit that I may be aflame. But flame is transient, often short-lived. Canst thou bear this, my soul—short life? In me there dwells the Spirit of the Great Short-Lived, whose zeal for God's house consumed Him. And he has promised baptism with the Spirit and with Fire. Make me Thy fuel, Flame of God.

  -James Elliot
  (SOA, pg. 158)

I indeed baptize you with water unto repentance: but he that cometh after me is mightier than I, whose shoes I am not worthy to bear: he shall baptize you with the Holy Ghost, and with fire (Matthew 3:11).

❖ This nominal Christian, who does not have the Spirit of God continually inspiring and working in him, has only a Christianity of his own making.

-William Law
(WRP, pg. 74)

❖ Man has no part in this redemption. He can only submit to the Holy Ghost to fully realize his inheritance. It is his submission to the Spirit of God that allows him to discover the unseen riches of Christ. It is the Holy Ghost who gives believers wisdom from above to recognize the nuggets of God in His Word and ways. It is the Spirit of God who unveils the mysteries of Christ that is veiled in His Written Word.

-RJK

That the God of our Lord Jesus Christ, the Father of glory, may give unto you the spirit of wisdom and revelation in the knowledge of him (Ephesians 1:17)

❖ God desires to create in our heart the childlike disposition so distasteful to the spirit of fallen man, but so agreeable to the spirit of the gospel.

-Fenelon

******

Lord, I'm a stranger here alone;
Earth no true comforts can afford:
Yet, absent from your dearest one,
My soul delights to cry, My Lord!
Jesus, my Lord, my only love,
Possess my soul, nor thence depart:

Grant me kind visits, heavenly Dove;
My God shall then have all My heart.

-David Brainerd
(LDD, pgs. 82, 83)

******

What Spirit Are You of?

Through the years I have struggled with why God does not step into a matter to somehow right it, or make it sweet to the soul of the saint. After all, He has all power at His disposal. In one swipe of His hand, He could change everything. However, God does not work according to His power, but in line with the sweet nature and temperance of His Spirit.

God is motivated and moved by His Spirit. This incredible understanding changed how I considered the intervention of God. He may be all powerful, but it is tempered by His Spirit. He may be Almighty, but His strength is under the meek control of His Spirit. Clearly, the Spirit brings clear discipline to the matters of heaven. Granted, He may do the Father's bidding and lead all believers to the reality of Christ, but He is the motivation, moving, and inspiration behind heaven.

From this premise I began to understand Jesus' words to John and James in Luke 9:55 when He rebuked them for their suggestion to rain fire from heaven on the Samaritans. He stated that they did not know what spirit they were of.

We are told that God would give us a new heart and spirit in relationship to the new covenant. As believers, we are instructed to try the spirits and make sure that we are following after, being led by, and walking in His Spirit.

There are many spirits in operation, but there is only one spirit that must motivate, move, and inspire us in our lives before God. It is the same Spirit who tempers the hand of God, motivates His heart, inspires His attitudes, and ensures the purity of His kingdom.

Then he answered and spake unto me, saying, This is the word of the LORD unto Zerubbabel, saying, Not by might, nor by power, but by my Spirit, saith the LORD of hosts (Zechariahs 4:6).

Wisdom and Knowledge

❖ There are three states of the soul—ignorance, opinion, knowledge—those who are in ignorance are the pagans (Gentiles), those in knowledge the true Church, and those in opinion, the Heretics.

-Clement of Alexandria
(GPQ, pg. 129)

❖ Knowledge is knowing a tomato is a fruit. Wisdom is not putting it in a fruit salad.

-Unknown

❖ A wise man is nothing more than a fool with a good memory.

-Unknown

❖ Let us not fool ourselves—without Christianity, without Christian education, without the principles of Christ inculcated into young life, we are simply rearing pagans.

-Peter Marshall
(JMM, pg. 155)

❖ The mind can form thoughts about God from the Bible and know all the doctrine of salvation, while the inner life does not have the power of God to save.

-Andrew Murray

❖ When men search for religious knowledge instead of seeking to know God, they end up embracing superstition and ignorance about God.

-RJK

Now as touching things offered unto idols, we know that we all have knowledge. Knowledge puffeth up, but charity edifieth (1 Corinthians 8:1).

- Sin draws the mind away from a duty, but entices the emotions.

  -John Owen
  (ST, pg. 59)

- All the technology does is allow men to sin in more ways, more often, with more sophistication.

  -Marv Rosenthal

- Some people have thought that the more science we have, the more religion can be discarded. But that is not so. Rather, the fact is that the more science we have, the more we need character-building religion.

  -Peter Marshall
  (JMM, pg.65)

- Oh, the ignorance of the world! How some empty outward forms, that may all be entirely selfish, mistaken for true religion, infallible evidence of it. The Lord pity a deluded world.

  -David Brainerd
  (LDD, pg. 327)

- Small minds can never handle great themes.

  -Jerome
  (GPQ, pg. 183

- Virtue united with knowledge is wisdom.

  -Lactantius
  (DCB, pg. 549)

- Without revelation, we are sightless, discerning nothing, regardless of how many spiritual ideas we develop or pursue. God greatly desires zealots, but He cannot use blind zealots.

  -Manfred Haller
  (CA, pg. 119)

For I bear them record that they have a zeal for God, but not according to knowledge. For they being ignorant of God's righteousness, and going about to establish their own righteousness, have not submitted themselves unto the righteousness of God (Romans 10:2-3).

- Obedience without knowledge is blind, and knowledge without obedience is lame.

  -Thomas Watson
  (PDC, 277)

- It is natural for man to become an expert or an authority in a matter that has not personally touched him, but let such a matter intrude into his life and you will see a different man. You will see someone who is apt to not only wallow in self-pity, but in anger and bitterness.

  -RJK

- We have two powers at work: the understanding or intellect which knows things from the ideas we form; and the heart which knows them by experience as they become part of our will and desires.

  -Andrew Murray

******

To experience Light
Is to illuminate
the way to go forward
each day.

A new journey
as life unfolds
a new step
day by day.

Wisdom from above
as a guiding Light
Joy unexpected,

fulfillment,
full,
no voids.

Old is young, and
Young is old.

Silvery are the hairs
of those who hold
that which is of
apples gold.

-Maureen Human

- The only intellectual power that can help to bring man again into the region of divine light, is that poor, despised thing called simplicity. Simplicity stops the workings of the fallen nature, and it leaves room for God to work again in the soul, according to the good pleasure of His holy will.

  -William Law
  (WRP, pg. 88)

- Unlearning is often the most important part of learning: wrong impressions, prejudices, and beliefs are obstacles in the way of learning until these have been removed, the teacher labors in vain.

  -Andrew Murray

But were mingled among the heathen, and learned their works. And they served their idols, which were a snare unto them (Psalm 106:35-36).

- The fountain of wisdom and religion is God. And if those two streams turn aside from Him, they will dry up. For those who are ignorant of Him cannot be wise or religious.

  -Lactantius
  (DCB, pg. 549)

- The Lord possesses wisdom. Therefore, wisdom existed from the beginning. It was involved in the creation of the world; therefore, we can see it in action. Those who are childlike in heart can hear it, and those who fear the Lord can know it. When wisdom is heard, it brings understanding to those pure in heart. When it is valued as gold, it brings instruction to those who seek it for its ways.

-RJK

Happy is the man that findeth wisdom, and the man that getteth understanding (Proverbs 3:13).

******

The Contrasts of Proverbs 31

Godly wisdom brings contrast to a matter by bringing forth practical contrasts. We see this contrast especially being brought out in Proverbs 30. A man by the name of Agur painted a decisive picture in regards to four types of contrasts that reveal the quality or character of a matter. For example, there are four things that are not able to be satisfied, the grave that embraces death, the barren womb that is devoid of life, the earth that lacks the water that refreshes, and fire that refuses to accept boundaries. This is truly a picture of man's soul.

There are four things too wonderful to describe, the eagle with its ability to gain heights, the serpent that will not be stopped by a rock, a ship that confronts the challenges of the water, and a man who cherishes the one he cares for. These contrasts show spiritual liberty and victory for those who possess God's perspective. Such individuals will not be stopped by worldly obstacles and currents when it comes to the matters of heaven, and what they have learned to truly value in light of the eternal.

There are four things that oppress a person's spirit, the servant who reins, the fool who is satisfied with the temporary, the ungodly woman who is married, and the immature who are heir to that which calls for discretion.

Agur shows four things that are wise, the ant who is diligent in life, the conies that show initiative, the locusts that show discretion, and the spider who is not intimidated.

There are also four things that are beautiful in their realm, the strength of the lion, the speed of the greyhound, the value or potential of the he goat, and a king against whom there is no opposition.

Mercy and Grace

- God is merciful. However, this mercy is expressed even in negative ways. Granted, He does not allow us to experience His wrath, but He does allow us to taste the bitter cup of adversity to bring inner discipline to our lives.

-RJK

- Here then is where the deceit of sin intervenes. It separates the doctrine of grace from its purpose. It persuades us to dwell upon the notion of grace and diverts our attention from the influence that grace gives to achieve its proper application in holy lives.

-John Owen
(ST, pg. 41)

My brethren, count it all joy when ye fall into divers temptations: Knowing this, that the trial of your faith worketh patience (James 1:2-3).

- Nothing so cultivates the grace of patience as the endurance of temptation, and nothing so drives the soul to an utter dependence upon the Lord Jesus as its continuance. And finally, nothing brings more praise and honor and glory to our Lord Himself than the trial of our faith that comes through manifold temptations.

-Hannah Whitall Smith

❖ The more we grow in grace, the more we shall flourish in glory.

-Thomas Watson

And of his fullness have all we received, and grace for grace (John 1:16).

❖ It is grace we need, and not sin, to make and keep us humble. The heaviest-laden branches always bow the lowest. The greatest flow of water makes the deepest river bed.

-Andrew Murray

❖ Mercy may seem slow, but it is sure.

-Charles Spurgeon
(FCB, pg. 316)

❖ This throne of grace is to be distinguished from all other thrones of God referred to in the Word. *The throne of His essential glory* is unapproachable by all creatures. *The throne of justice* is dreadful to the sinner. We should pray against coming before this throne. . . There is also *the throne of the Judge at the last day.* But this throne is not yet set up, though it will surely be; we know not how soon, so we should prepare for our appearing before it. But this *throne of grace* is the gracious manifestation of God in Christ, reconciling the world to Himself.

-Robert Traill

Let us therefore come boldly unto the throne of grace, that we may obtain mercy, and find grace to help in time of need (Hebrews 4:16).

❖ In the life of grace, forgiveness is one of the first blessings we receive from God.

-Andrew Murray

❖ The Apostle Paul presented the work of grace throughout his epistles. Today, grace is either being abused or frustrated, but few in Christendom seem to understand how it works. People's ignorance about grace is a product of not understanding the nature of God and how sin has personally affronted His character and cost Him His only begotten Son. For example, grace abounds at the point of repentance, never at the point of practicing sin. It meets us in our weakness, never in our arrogance. We can only acquire this grace through faith that properly responds to God, never through good works. We have been called into this grace, and it is by grace that we are partakers of all that God has for us. In other words, everything that is good and worthwhile comes from God, which is a matter of His grace. It is not a product of personal attempts or of so-called "goodness".

-RJK

What shall we say then? Shall we continue in sin, that grace may abound? God forbid. How shall we, that are dead to sin, live any longer in it (Romans 6:1-2)?

❖ Men may fall by sin, but cannot raise up themselves without the help of grace.

-John Bunyan

❖ The grace of God does not find men fit for salvation, but makes them so.

-Augustine
(GPQ, pg. 119)

❖ Therein I am made aware for two great forces for good in human experience: the fear of God and the grace of God. Without the fear of God I would not stop at doing evil; for fear of God restrains. Without the grace of God I would have no desire to approach positive goodness. The one is a deterrent from evil; the other is an encouragement to good.

-James Elliot
(SOA, pgs. 155, 156)

- Just as writing pen or a dart has need of one to employ it, so also does grace have need of believing hearts...It is God's part to confer grace, but ours to accept and guard it.

  -Cyril of Jerusalem
  (GPQ, pg. 122)

- Either let us fear the wrath to come or let us value the grace we have: one or the other.

  -Ignatius
  (GPQ. pg. 123)

- We live in a dispensation of grace. This dispensation does not allow us to live as we choose, but to experience God's mercy in our lives and to know His faithfulness in our times of need. After all, God's longsuffering towards us is not for the purpose of hiding behind some concept of grace, but to give us time to repent, so that, out of grace, He can intervene on our behalf.

  -RJK

If ye have heard of the dispensation of the grace of God which is given me to you-ward (Ephesians 3:2).

Life in the Spirit

Love

- Everything which relates to God is infinite. We must therefore, while we keep our hearts humble, keep our aims high. Our highest services are indeed but finite, imperfect. But as God is unlimited in goodness, He should have our unlimited love.

  - Hannah More

- The life of the world is self-pleasing and self-exalting. The life of heaven is holy, self-denying love.

  -Andrew Murray

A new commandment I give unto you, That ye love one another; as I have loved you, that ye also love one another (John 13:34).

- When we each come to this place of completeness, we will discover that what remains standing will be a product of genuine faith, a reality of the unending hope of heaven, and the incredible, enduring character and work of God's charity. When we realize that we will be discovering how the grace distributed according to God's charity has truly benefitted our lives, we will come to one distinct conclusion. All that is attached to faith, hope, and charity will forever abide, but the greatest of these three will forever resonate through the corridors of our spirits as we are reminded throughout eternity that "God so loved each of us, He gave His only begotten Son."

  -RJK

And now abideth faith, hope, charity, these three; but the greatest of these is charity (1 Corinthians 13:13).

- The cross which conforms you into His image is a consoling bond of love between you and Him.

  -Fenelon
  (SH, pg. 9)

- Without the holiness which pleases God, we cannot please Jesus. He who cares nothing for holiness knows nothing of the love of Jesus.

  -Charles Spurgeon

- Consider the sinful woman who wet Jesus' feet with her tears—she was forgiven, "for she loved much." True love will give up its life for a brother. This is the mark, the primary evidence of God's Church.

  -Manfred Haller

Wherefore I say unto thee, Her sins, which are many, are forgiven; for she loved much: but to whom little is forgiven, the same loveth little (Luke 7:47).

- If I am content to heal a hurt slightly, saying "Peace, peace," where is no peace; if I forget the poignant word "Let love be without dissimulation" and blunt the edge of truth, speaking not right things but smooth things, then I know nothing of Calvary love.

  -Amy Carmichael

******

Why have I not a thousand
thousands hearts,
Lord of my Soul — that they
might all be Thine?
If THOU approve — the zeal Thy
smile imparts,

How should it ever fail? Can such
a fire decline?
Love, pure and holy, is a deathless
fire, —
Its object heavenly,— it must ever
blaze!
Eternal Love a God must needs
Inspire,
When once He wins the heart, and
Fits it for His praise!

-Madam Guyon

❖ There is a tremendous liberty in godly love. Since it is honorable, it does not have to keep up a façade about its intentions. It is sacrificial; therefore, it is dead to self-serving agendas and jealousies, making it ready to fling off all matters pertaining to this world to bring glory to that which is heavenly. Such a love has the touch of eternity; therefore, it is enduring and faithful.

-RJK

❖ If we believe in Jesus, it is not what we gain but what He pours through us that really counts. God's purpose is not simply to make us beautiful, plump grapes, but to make us grapes so that He may squeeze the sweetness out of us.

-Oswald Chambers

******

God, Thou Art Love

If I forget,
Yet God remembers! If these hands of mine
Cease from their clinging, yet the hands divine
Hold me so firmly that I cannot fail;

And if sometimes I am too tired to call
    For Him to help me, then He reads the prayer
Unspoken in my heart, and lifts my care.

I dare not fear, since certainly I know
    That I am in God's keeping, shielded so
From all that else would harm, and in the hours
    Of stern temptation strengthened by His power;
I tread no path in life to Him unknown;
    I lift no burden, bear no pain, alone:
My soul a calm, sure hiding-place has found:
    The everlasting arms my life surround.

God, Thou art love! I build my faith on that,
    I know Thee who has kept my path, made
Light for me in the darkness, tempering sorrow
    So that it reached me like a solemn joy;
It were too strange that I should doubt Thy love.

-Robert Browning
(HFG, pg. 25)

- My friend, Maureen Human, noted in her journal that one day she and her grandson found a grasshopper among the strawberries. The little creature appeared to be cold. Maureen picked up the leaf that it was on, and moved it to a place where the rays of the sun could enfold the creature into its warmth. Within minutes it jumped off. She noted in her journal that the unfolding events of the grasshopper reminded her that we all need the warmth of God's love in our lives so we may be moved to action.

- Fear without love remains fear. However, love that walks in a proper attitude of fear towards the Lord will express itself in wisdom, honor, awe, and worship.

-RJK

There is no fear in love; but perfect love casteth out fear: because fear hath torment, He that feareth is not made perfect in love (1 John 4:18).

- By this providence we may see that sin is the worst of evils, for sickness came with sin. Christ is the chief good; therefore, let us love him. Sin is the worst of evils, therefore, let us hate that with a perfect hatred.

  -Matthew Henry

- The purest of all loves is a will so filled with the will of God that there remains nothing else.

  -Fenelon
  (TWG, pg. 114)

Herein is love, not that we loved God, but that he loved us, and sent his Son to be the propitiation for our sins (1 John 4:10).

- The hidden unity of life must be manifest in the visible unity and fellowship of love.

  -Andrew Murray

- True love only rejoices in truth, not in iniquity. If you walk in love, you will not ignore sin on a personal level or when it affects others. Love will contend for the souls of those enslaved by sin. Such love is minus judgmentalism, and has one goal--restoration. It is separate from the ways of the world, meek in its approach, discreet in its conduct, and wise in how it contends with those who are enslaved.

  -RJK

Rejoiceth not in iniquity, but rejoiceth in the truth (1 Corinthians 13:6).

- Christlike obedience is the way to a Christlike enjoyment of divine love.

  -Andrew Murray

- You have your joys where you have your longings...He who does not fear to lose, does not find it difficult to give.

  -Tertullian

- The more you selfishly love yourself, the more critical you will be.

  -Fenelon

******

The Door of Opportunity

Jesus is clear that people will know we are His disciples because we possess godly love. Such love is unfeigned and sacrificial. It is quick to step past the convenience of self and avail itself to that which is not beneficial or pleasant. The reason for this is because godly love is not selfish and is always looking for an opportunity to express itself for the glory of God.

I know that we emphasize that which we love enough we put a value on it. For example, we witness the extent of God's love on the old rugged cross. He so valued us that He gave the best. His Son so loved He sacrificed all. The expression and action of true love can be clearly seen on this altar established by God 20 centuries ago.

If we possess the same love of God, we can do no less when it comes to expressing it. The problem with most of us is the love we possess is conditional for it is directed at self. It will only love that which might serve its purpose. The main goal of such selfish love is to feel good about itself in its utter abyss of darkness and despair. It wants to be served rather than serve. It wants to look good instead of being honorable in its commitment and actions. It wants to perceive that it is worthy of adoration, rather than become humble by its worthless, insipid ways in light of God's love.

Selfish love is prideful; therefore, it is very unrealistic about how it must be treated, critical of that which will not serve it, cruel towards that which will not recognize it, and full of self-pity when disillusioned. The fruits of this self-love can be seen in some of the attitudes that exist in what I refer to as "American Christianity."

Radio and TV host Glenn Beck put it best when he stated that instead of the common ground of agreement for many Americans being that of wise, godly principles established by God and upheld by our founding fathers, it has become stuff. This fickle, fragile common ground will be defeated by ideology regardless how wicked it is.

From this observation the harsh reality is that many Americans have put a high price on stuff. As I pondered this reality, I began to understand why so many Americans, including Christians, value stuff. They can hide behind and in it. They can literally become lost in it to such an extent they can ignore reality and responsibility as they slide by in their lives. Meanwhile, they can become indifferent to the needs of others, clueless to the winds of judgment pounding against the dark tombs of their small, depressing worlds, and justified as to the cruelty they display because they lack true benevolence.

This was recently brought to the forefront in my life. I was involved in helping a particular person disperse of some household goods. This person carried the handle of being a "Christian." An individual had spotted something that he desired. He carefully studied it and handled it with such longing. He asked the price on it. The "Christian" gave the man a price. He walked up looking in his billfold, counting the money; however, he was a few dollars short. He admitted it, but to my surprise, the person was not moved at all. This "Christian" did not seem to care that the man had such a deep desire for it and that a few dollars would not make any difference in the quality of her life. It was clearly "stuff" to the person, but a desired treasure to this man. It was a great opportunity for this woman to become a witness by showing compassion and displaying the benevolence of a Christian to this man, but instead, she lamely justified away her indifferent attitude as she remained stubborn and unmoved in her position.

At the time, I was so shocked by the indifference of this person that I was paralyzed by it. I would have had no problem making up the difference or paying the whole price for it if necessary to make sure he did not short himself. However, by the time I gained my composure, the man had left.

That night my soul was in grave distress. I realized that through life we have been given small windows of opportunity to do good to others in a spirit of true benevolence. Such opportunities will quickly come and go, and only godly love will be prepared to avail itself in sincere benevolence to not only recognize the opportunity, but be prepared to naturally respond in a caring way.

As I struggled with the whole scene, I was reminded that the quality of our benevolence will always be tested in small ways. The man could have been an angel testing this woman's love. Her opportunity to show compassion to a stranger may have come in an insignificant way, but quickly the door slammed shut, leaving a bitter taste behind. Clearly, she miserably failed the test.

God chose a small window or door of opportunity to send His Son. Can you imagine the bitterness and hopelessness in each of our souls if He had ignored this window of opportunity for His Son to come? Can you imagine where we would be if God did not possess the benevolence He does? We would still be tasting the bitterness of being hopelessly lost to everything that has been marked by the glorious reality of Christ's redemption.

But whosoever hath this world's good, and seeth his brother have need, and shutteth up his bowels of compassion from him, how dwelleth the love of God in him? My little children, let us not love in world, neither in tongue, but in deed and in truth (1 John 3:17-18).

Christian Virtues

- Someone once said, "The grand essentials of happiness are: something to do, something to love, and something to hope for." As believers, we must realize that only the Lord can give us sustaining purpose, abiding love, and serve as the essence of all hope. It is only when Jesus takes His rightful place in our lives that we can truly experience the sweet fruits of lasting happiness.

  -RJK

- We are now at the place where we see that progress simply must be made in the realm of morals and ethics and character, if civilization is to be saved.

  -Peter Marshall
  (JMM, pg. 66)

- The wounds of conscience though generally received in public, must always be healed in private.

  -Herbert Lockyer
  (MP, pg. 163)

- Calamity is very often the discipline of virtue.

  -Mark Minucius Felix
  (DCB, pg. 548)

- Goodness is not benevolent and kind but genuine and true.

  -F. B. Meyer

- Only request on my behalf that I may not merely be called a Christian, but may really be found to be one.

  -Ignatius
  (DCB, pg. 547)

- The true Christian is uncomfortable in surroundings that are not in harmony with heavenly things.

  -Paris Reidhead
  (FRG, pg. 80)

- God is not concerned about our happiness but about our holiness. In other words, God is concerned that we wear character.

  -Leonard Ravenhill

- Virtue is not the knowing of good and evil. Rather, virtue is the doing of good and not doing of evil.

  -Lactantius
  (GPQ, pg. 284)

- There would have been no eloquent Peter at Pentecost had there been no humble Andrew to bring him to Jesus.

  -Dr. Claude McKay
  (JMM, pg. 54)

- The reality of greatness will be based on the type of witness it will leave behind. Often times such a legacy of greatness is riddled with what appears to be failure. However, it is in times of what appears to be utter failure that immense opportunity presents itself. The opportunity I speak of has to do with the forging of character that comes with adversity. To me, much of what we might deem as success comes from learning what not to do verses what to do. However, a person cannot learn what not to do unless he or she is willing to fail in the process of doing.

  -RJK

- These are the traits of character most sorely needed in our world today—a willingness to play second fiddle or, if you prefer, humility, and that broad sympathy and sound commonsense, without which the success of any great movement cannot be measured.

-Peter Marshall
(JMM, pg. 59)

- Man can accomplish anything he wants if he doesn't mind who gets the credit.

-President Ronald Reagan

- If you want big instead of better, you will always end up with the oyster instead of the pearl.

-Jeannette Haley

- When it comes to the world we live in, greatness is always born out of the ordinary. It never begins from that which is already considered great to the world, but from that which is considered foolish, base, and despised. It is from this premise that real greatness is realized.

-RJK

- If ever man becomes proud, let him remember that a gnat preceded him in the divine order of creation!

Tosefta, Sanhedrin 88

In like manner, ye younger, submit yourselves unto the elder. Yea, all of you be subject one to another, and be clothed with humility; for God resisteth the proud, and giveth grace to the humble (1 Peter 5:5).

- Man was created with two eyes, so that with one he may see God's greatness, and with the other his own lowliness.

-Samuel J. Agnon

- You will either be abased or exalted by God. The issue of abasement and exaltation *always* rests at the feet of humility.

-RJK

- Nothing is more scandalous than a man that is proud of his humility.

-Marcus Aurelius
(MP, pg. 141)

- Be extremely distrustful of your intellect and your own ideas of perfection. That will be a great step toward becoming perfect. Humility and distrust of yourself, with simplicity, are fundamental virtues for you.

-Fenelon

- He humbled Himself as low as humiliation could go in order to love and to bless me.

-Andrew Murray

******

The voice is in the breeze
as the stars go winkling by,
Blue azure clear glass,
see who you are in Him.
Truly wonderful
an image of He.
Naked, plain,
unmasked
unadorned
see who you are—
humbly come to Him
and let Him
cover you with
His righteousness.
Beautiful!
In His eyes are you
Bought with the glorious
blood of the Lamb.

-Maureen Human

And I beheld, and, lo, in the midst of the throne and of the four beasts, and in the midst of the elders, stood a Lamb as it had been slain, having seven horns and seven eyes, which are the seven Spirits of God sent forth into all the earth (Revelation 5:6).

- I never felt it so sweet to be nothing, and less than nothing, and to be accounted nothing.

  -David Brainerd
  (LDD, pg. 87)

- The most *lowly* Christian--is **the most *lovely* Christian!**

  -William Dyer

Verily I say unto you, Whosoever shall not receive the kingdom of God as a little child shall in no wise enter it (Luke 18:17).

- God give me a deep humility, a well-guided zeal, a burning love and a single eye, and then let men or devils do their worst.

  -George Whitefield

- Fenelon tells us there are two things that produce humility in us: the realization that the all-powerful hand of God has snatched us from the abyss of personal wretchedness, and the presence of the God who is becoming the ALL in all matters of life.

- It is hard to make people realize that, in communion with God, our attitude and character means everything. A meek and lowly heart is the very seed and root of all Christian character.

  -Andrew Murray

- Let me learn by paradox
  that the way down is the way up,
  that to be low is to be high,
  that the broken heart is the healed heart,
  that the contrite spirit is the rejoicing spirit,
  that the repenting soul is the victorious soul,
  that to have nothing is to possess all,
  that to bear the cross is to wear the crown,

that to give is to receive,
that the valley is the place of vision.

-Collection of Puritan Prayers and Devotions.

- Nothing is as important as lowliness of heart, and detachment from your own opinion and will. Stiffness and harshness are not the spirit of Jesus Christ.

-Fenelon

- Humility is the root, mother, nurse, foundation, and bond of all virtue.

-John Chrysostom
(GPQ, 140)

- If we are to be as the image of the heavenly Christ in glory, we must first bear the image of the earthly Christ in humility.

-Andrew Murray
(LC, pg. 225)

And as we have borne the image of the earthly (Adam), we shall also bear the image of the heavenly (1 Corinthians 15:49). (Parentheses added.)

- Especially, I discoursed repeatedly on the nature and necessity of that humiliation, self-emptiness, or full conviction of a person's being utterly undone in himself, which is necessary in order to a saving faith, and the extreme difficulty of being brought to this, and the great danger there is of persons taking up with some self-righteous appearances of it. The danger of this I especially dwelt upon, being persuaded that multitudes perish in this hidden way; and because so little is said from most pulpits to discover any danger here; so that persons being never effectually brought to die in themselves are never truly united to Christ, and so perish.

-David Brainerd
(LDD, pg. 354)

Having a form of godliness, but denying the power thereof: from such turn away (2 Timothy 3:5).

- Always fear haughtiness. Fear overconfidence in your own ideas, and determination in your way of speaking. Be meek and humble in heart.

-Fenelon
(TWG, pg. 15)

- Meekness is the opposite of all that is hard, bitter, or sharp. It refers to the disposition that makes us compassionate towards others.

-Andrew Murray
(LC, pg, 185)

- He that is down needs fear no fall, He that is low no pride.

-John Bunyan

Wherefore let him that thinketh he standeth take heed lest he fall (1 Corinthians 10:12).

- Vision looks inward and becomes duty. Vision looks outward and becomes aspiration. Vision looks upward and becomes faith.

-Stephen S. Wise

- People can correctly speak about the character of God, but remain quite limited in understanding His ways. The reason people fail to come to an understanding of God is that they consider the circumstances that befall man, rather than the mysterious reality of God. In other words, there is so much that we do not know about God's reasoning behind what He does or His purpose for a matter. This is why faith plays an important part in our walk. Faith towards God must be applied when we do not understand the whys of our life.

-RJK

- But the Kingdom is a venture of faith—not doubt. It is a matter of perception—not of proof.

-Peter Marshall
(JMM, pg. 41)

- Faith honors God. God honors faith and goes wherever faith puts Him.

  -Leonard Ravenhill
  (RPR, pg. 28)

- Faith will lead you in; experience will teach you; Scripture will train you...

  -Clement of Alexandria
  (GPQ, pg. 98)

- Where reason cannot wade there faith may swim.

  -Thomas Watson

- For the new Christian, he or she must choose to walk by faith. The faith walk means making the decision to obey the Word of God because of who He is. Such obedience will lead the individual through deep valleys of temptation, up foreboding mountains of challenges, and into wildernesses of uncertainty. In fact, everything about the Christian walk will make the Christian life seem full of drudgery at times, while proving to be unpredictable at others. The Christian life is not dependent on the terrain or the surroundings, but on the immovable Rock that never sways from its eternal character and foundation.

  -RJK

- No faith that is exercised in the future tense amounts to anything...The enemy delights in this future faith, for he knows it is powerless to accomplish any practical results.

  -Hannah Whitall Smith

- Only faith empties us of our own self-sufficiency. We should not live to ourselves, but only for Christ, by Christ and in Christ.

  -John Owen

- Humble love, not proud reason, keeps the door of heaven. May we, therefore, condescend to things of low estate, experiencing the power of the lowly one Himself in overcoming our pride with His humility!

-Herbert Lockyer
(MP, pg. 142)

Be of the same mind one toward another. Mind not high things, but condescend to men of low estate. Be not wise in your own conceits (Romans 12:16).

- As you follow Abraham, you will see a man that matured in his faith. His faith started out as a mustard seed, was made simple in its purity through obedience, and materialized in a friendship with God.

-RJK

- Faith's way of gaining is giving.

-Charles Spurgeon

- When faith ceases to pray it ceases to live.

-Leonard Ravenhill
(RPR, pg. 33)

- Fainting is more apt to occur in the valleys of daily drudgery than on the pinnacles of public performance. The real test of our faith will always be in the dark valleys where we cannot perceive God's presence. It is there we question our calling, our capabilities, and our commitment.

-Jeannette Haley

- We need a faith that is as real as fire. . . and prayer as real as potatoes.

-Peter Marshall
(JMM, pg. 176)

- Faith is in the custody of a gallant heart; timidity always surrenders to a brave spirit.

-E. M. Bounds
(WOP, pg. 147)

- Did not the righteous Job question the matters surrounding God and life? It surprises me how believers act as if real faith will never question God. Real faith will question in search to understand the ways of God. It seeks out the character and work of God in a matter. Such a search is about finding the heart and will of God about a situation. At times faith can become impatient in the fiery test, only to find peace as it is stretched to embrace more of the reality of God.

-RJK

Wherefore, I was grieved with that generation, and said, They do always err in their heart, and they have not known my ways (Hebrews 3:10).

- God wants to build a relationship with you that is based on faith and trust and not on glamorous miracles.

-Fenelon
(SH, pg. 25)

******

Big Brown eyes
Looking at you.
Loneliness settled in.
Despair all around.
Whispering hope,
whispering—
softness, trusting
this voice I hear.
It is all I need.
It is sufficient
to meet my needs.
It will all be
explained someday
up in the sky.

-Maureen Human

❖ Do you not know that the step of faith always "falls on the seeming void, but finds the rock beneath"?

-Hannah Whitall Smith

❖ Our Father, remove from us sophistication of our age and the skepticism that has come, like frost, to blight our faith and to make it weak. Bring us back to a faith that makes us great and strong, a faith that enables us to love and to live, the faith by which we are triumphant, and the faith by which alone we can walk with Thee. We pray for a return of that simple faith, that old-fashioned trust in God, that made strong and great the homes of our ancestors who built this good land and who in building left us our heritage.

-Peter Marshall
(JMM, pg. 159)

❖ Someone has said that faith has *three* distinct stages: the faith that *reckons*, the faith that *rests*, the faith that *risks*. (RPR, pg. 54)

So we see that they could not enter in because of unbelief (Hebrews 3:19).

❖ Jesus calls us into a life that He oversees, not one we control. He calls us into the unknown that we will not understand or feel comfortable in. But, if we are going to gain our life in Christ, we must follow Him into uncharted territories.

-RJK

❖ Through the channel of faith comes all that we have or ever will have in the Christian life this side of eternity.

-Leonard Ravenhill
(RPR, pg.163)

❖ The benefit that we receive from faith is the power and presence of God living and working in our beings.

-William Law
(WRP, pg. 4)

- As believers, we must remember that, on the great day of judgment when all will be stripped from each of us, only the pure gold of unfeigned faith, the refined silver of redemption that has been tried in the fires of testing and separation, and the precious stones of our loving devotion will survive the penetrating fire of His holy judgment upon all of that which has been truly committed to Him by faith.

-RJK

Every man's work shall be made manifest: for the day shall declare it, because it shall be revealed by fire; and the fire shall try every man's work of what sort it is. If any man's work abide which he hath built thereupon, he shall receive a reward (1 Corinthians 3:13-14).

- Those who are God's true witnesses are firmly anchored in Him, in love or in suffering, no matter what God may give or take away. They do not set much store by their own methods; if they prove helpful to their spiritual life, well and good. But God, in his loving foresight, often shatters their foundations and thus they frequently find themselves thwarted. If they want to keep vigil, they are obliged to sleep; if they like to fast, they are made to eat; if they would like to keep silence and be at rest, they have to do otherwise. In this way, everything they cleave to crumbles, and they are brought face-to-face with their bare nothingness. Thus they are shown how total is their dependence on God, and they learn to confess Him with a pure and simple faith, with no other support to sustain them.

-Johannes Tauler

- A living faith in His eternal purpose will become one of the mightiest powers in urging and helping us to live like Christ.

-Andrew Murray

For unto us was the gospel preached, as well as unto them: but the word preached did not profit them, not being mixed with faith in them that heard it (Hebrews 4:2).

- By knowing God, one is able to stand on His character and withstand according to His promises.

  -RJK

That ye be not slothful, but followers of them who through faith and patience inherit the promises (Hebrews 6:12).

- There is no doubt that the life of faith is the most penetrating of all deaths.

  -Fenelon
  (SH, pg. 7)

- He who in faith surrenders himself to be filled with Him will experience how gloriously He accomplishes His work of stamping the image and likeness of Christ on our souls and lives.

  -Andrew Murray

- For faith to produce a greater quality of character in the believer, it must, in a sense, be conceived in the darkness of uncertainty, birthed in sorrow, and brought forth to maturity in pain, despair, and hopelessness.

  -RJK

- The prayer closet is the garden of faith.

  -E. M. Bounds

- God does not expect us to submit our faith to Him without reason, but the very limits of our reason make faith a necessity.

  -Augustine
  (GPQ, pg. 96)

- True faith towards the character of God can only be put into practice when present matters do not make sense, and there is nothing on the horizon that implies that the ship of reason and the calm waters of order will return to our world any time soon.

  -RJK

- Nothing is harder to heal than a broken heart shattered by experiences that seem so meaningless. But God's people don't live on explanations; God's people live on His promise.

  -Warren Wiersbe

- Without faith every human labor is empty.

  -Fulgence of Ruspe
  (GPQ, pg. 96)

And he that doubeth is damned if he eat, because he eateth not of faith: for what ever is not of faith is sin (Romans 14:23).

- Faith is the sight of the soul. It is the eyes of the human spirit, the ability to see what is not there yet—to see what's going to be there.

  -Paris Reidhead
  (FRG. Pg. 95)

- Faith leads us to the calm waters of God's sovereign grace and protection.

  -RJK

- A friend... said, "You were healed by faith." "Oh, no," I said, "I was healed by Christ." What is the difference? There is a great difference. There came a time when even faith seemed to come between me and Jesus. I thought I should have to work up the faith, so I laboured to get the faith. At last I thought I had it; that if I put my whole weight upon it, it would hold. I said, when I thought I had got the faith, "Heal me." I was trusting in myself, in my own heart, in my own faith. I was asking the Lord to do something for me because of something in me, not because of something in Him.

  -A.B. Simpson

But without faith it is impossible to please him: for he that cometh to God must believe that he is, and that he is a rewarder of them that diligently seek him (Hebrews 11:6).

- God is not looking for brilliant men, is not depending upon eloquent men, is not shut up to the use of talented men in sending His gospel out in the world. God is looking for broken men who have judged themselves in the light of the cross of Christ. When He wants anything done, He takes up men who have come to the end of themselves, whose confidence is not in themselves, but in God.

-H. A. Ironside

- The Spirit of God first sows the seed of divine union in the soul of a man. Then afterward, faith revives the seed, raises it up, and brings it forth to a fullness of life in God.

  -William Law
  (WRP, pg. 12)

- Christians must not forget that there is a great war between righteousness and wickedness. In between this battle stands our faith. We must wrestle with the frontal attacks that would change our perception of God, take our sword of His Word to the seductive attempts of the enemy to change our reality, and keep our helmet of salvation in place when heresy bombards us with its deception. It is up to us to contend for our faith, knowing that God never changes, His Word stands sure, and His righteous ways lead to deliverance.

  -RJK

Beloved, when I gave all diligence to write unto you of the common salvation, it was needful for me to write unto you, and exhort you that ye should earnestly contend for the faith which was once delivered unto the saints (Jude 3).

- Faith and obedience always are the same thing—two sides of the same coin.

  -Paris Reidhead
  (FRG, pg. 96)

- There is a difference between *standing upright before* God and *being upright in* God. The latter recognizes that God alone is the source of all righteousness.

  -RJK

- Faith and godliness...are so closely allied that they can be considered sisters.

  -Athanasius
  (GPQ, pg. 97)

- The One who is righteous and holy has actually created us to operate in holiness. Holiness is a state that is maintained by the right attitude: that of fearing God. We are to walk according to the ways of holiness: that of righteousness, and our behavior should express the influence of holiness in our lives through godliness. The holy state allows a person to actually come into agreement with God about the matters of heaven and life.

  -RJK

Follow peace with all men, and holiness, without which no man shall see the Lord (Hebrews 12:14).

- He who is ignorant of God must also be ignorant of justice.

  -Lactantius

- Inward evil can only be cured or overcome by an inward good.

  -William Law

- Men are indeed fickle when it comes to the God of heaven. The reason for this fickleness is that they want righteousness on their terms and not God's.

  -RJK

- Because God's Word is food, bread from heaven, the first reason for Bible study is: a great hunger for righteousness—a great desire to do all God's will.

  -Andrew Murray
  (DEG, pg. 42)

Blessed are they who do hunger and thirst after righteousness: for they shall be filled (Matthew 5:6).

- ❖ The natural response of godliness is the readiness to do good works for the glory of God.

-RJK

******

The Prophetic Side of Righteousness

In the book, *Seven Miracles that Saved America*, the authors Chris and Ted Stewart related a story about President Ronald Reagan. In 1970 while he was yet governor of California, he was visited one Sunday afternoon by his longtime friend Pat Boone, and some other prominent religious leaders. Since he was up for reelection, no doubt one of the subjects they were there to talk and pray about was his upcoming election.

As they joined hands, a Christian businessman by the name of George Otis was prompted to speak by the Holy Spirit. What Otis related to the group proved to be prophetic. It revealed that God is truly involved with the affairs of man, history, politics, and the future. He declared, "My son, if you walk uprightly before Me, you will reside at 1600 Pennsylvania Avenue."

Although, many in the liberal circles have mocked the actor who became President ten years later, there is no doubt that his time in the White House was ordained by God. As President, Reagan had the moral character and the wisdom to face the financial crisis and take on the international environment that was present. As a result, he was able to change the face of the predominate politics of his era. The beauty of God is that He takes the unlikely, calls them to Himself, forges them into what is considered excellent, and uses them to do the incredible.

******

❖ Righteousness is God's hatred of sin and maintenance of the righteous. Holiness is God's glory, in the perfect harmony of His righteousness and love.

-Andrew Murray

And the LORD said unto Satan, Hast thou considered my servant Job, that there is none like him in the earth, a perfect and an upright man, one that feareth God, and eschewed evil (Job 1:8)?

❖ An upright relationship with God keeps us dependent on Him, teachable before Him, and honorable in Him.

-RJK

❖ The highest perfection and the deepest mystery of the Godhead is His holiness. In it, righteousness and love are united.

-Andrew Murray

(LC, pg. 213)

❖ Many people know how to be a "character" in life, but few possesses true character.

-RJK

❖ The soul that has chosen the best life—the life that is from God and righteousness—exchanges earth for heaven.

-Clement of Alexandria
(DCB, pg. 547)

But seek ye first the kingdom of God, and his righteousness; and all these things shall be added unto you (Matthew 6:33).

❖ Have you ever noticed how people want you to take their side in a matter? I have long discovered that everyone believes their take on a matter makes them right. However, I have learned that the only way a person can be right is by being on the right side of God. This is and always will be a dividing line between the delusion of self-righteousness and possessing right standing in the kingdom of God.

-RJK

- To love means loving the unlovable. To forgive means pardoning the unpardonable. Faith means believing the unbelievable. Hope means hoping when everything seems hopeless.

  -Gilbert K. Chesterton

- Our greatest example of one who waited was Jesus Christ. He waited in eternity for His time to intrude into history. He waited in obscurity as He was prepared to walk though this world as the Son of Man and the Son of God. He waited in the night in prayer to gain strength. He waited in a garden for His accusers. He waited on the cross so that redemption could be completed. He waited in the bowels of the earth for the time He would be resurrected in newness. Now He waits in heaven for the time when He will be united with His Bride.

  -RJK

But let patience have her perfect work, that ye may be perfect and entire, wanting nothing (James 1:4).

- It is better to wait upon God with patience than to put confidence in any thing in this lower world.

  -David Brainerd
  (LDD, pg. 145)

******

Let us then hand in hand, walk
with Him who knows the way.
A peace that only He can give,
sustains us here on earth—a
training ground for that hope
which is to come. Alleluia—
Praise His name!

-Maureen Human

Peace I leave with you, my peace I give unto you: not as the world giveth, give I unto you. Let not your heart be troubled, neither let it be afraid (John 14:27).

Suffering and Sacrifice

- Every Christian church that does not teach its members the main religious science, sufferology, does not fulfill its duties. Impose upon yourself mortification. Learn to suffer and not to yield. The time may come when you will need this knowledge.

  -Richard Wurmbrand

- Martyr is defined as an associate of Christ's passion in Christ's name.

  -Letter to Cyprian
  From certain presbyters

- The Lord Jesus' incarnation was a self-sacrifice. His life of self-denial was the proof of it.

  -Andrew Murray

- That which is priceless comes with a price. Obviously, it takes tribulation to purify, refine, and fine-tune God's people to possess the priceless life of Christ. Therefore, how can Christians believe there will be no challenges in discovering the fullness of God in their lives?

  -RJK

Confirming the souls of the disciples, and exhorting them to continue in the faith, and that we must through much tribulation enter into the kingdom of God (Acts 14:22).

- The saints, however, do not wither in the face of trials.

  -Athanasius
  (GPQ, pg. 17)

******

The Sweet Ovens of Persecution

In America, we have enjoyed religious freedom, but such freedom has cost us our sense as to the value we possess because of it. As a result, unfeigned liberty has been abused, neglected, and scoffed at. Sadly, the consequences for such an attitude will be the loss of that precious freedom.

The reason most people fail to hold onto freedom is because they do not understand the nature of it. Those who are ignorant about freedom equate it with doing whatever they please, without paying consequences. However, such practices do not constitute real freedom. Rather, such actions speak of lawlessness and foolishness. With or without freedom wrong decisions and actions will result in unpleasant consequences. The unpleasant outcomes have to do with the natural law of reaping what is sown.

When we consider true liberty, it has to do with the freedom to do as our conscience dictates in relationship to morality and pure religion. If oppression exits, it will exit in these two arenas. Evil cannot afford to be exposed by the purity or light of that which is moral and upright. Such exposure would unveil its deception to rob, kill, and destroy what may stand in the way of its wicked agendas.

Much of the universal Bride of Christ understands the dark curtain of oppression. Whether it is in Communist countries or Muslim controlled countries, the voice of religious conscience, reason, and decency is being put into the oven of persecution in the name of God, Allah, government, tolerance, Social Justice, or humanism.

There are many incredible stories of the miraculous intervention of God on behalf of His persecuted Church. Such intervention can cause the fires of the ovens of persecution to become sweet to His saints.

I have read many such stories. Take the case of the Chinese woman who had her life turned upside down after the authorities came for her husband. They had been an evangelistic team together, but now he was being taken away with the threat by the officials that he would never return to her.

She was left alone to support their six children. It required her to work long days, and if that was not enough, she was often taken during the night for interrogations that ended just in time for her to put in another full day of work. She was even faced with temptation as the government encouraged her to divorce her husband while a gentleman waited in the wings to take her as his wife with the promise of making her life easy.

However, she did not feel released from her husband. The Lord assured her that he was alive. How long would this woman wait for her husband? Miraculously he was released, but it was 21 years later. She had believed the Lord, remained true to her husband, and was able to happily receive him back into their home without any regret or shame.

There was also the case of the Chinese woman doctor. Because of her faith half of her hair was shaved off and eventually she was demoted from her position as a doctor to clean the floors and latrines of the hospital. Even though she was married, she had to live in the basement of the hospital. She joyfully did her job for eleven years as unto her Lord. Her joy caused others to ask her about her attitude. She was able share the source behind her joy.

A year after Chairman Mao's death, the doctor was allowed to go home. Not only was she allowed to go home to her family, but she was awarded full back pay for the years she had lost from her profession. The amount she was paid was $13,000.00. The money helped sustain her family as well as ensured an education for her children.

In another situation, a dear saintly Chinese believer was able to use the confiscation of all the Bibles and religious materials as an opportunity to drop off the Jesus movie to the police station. She commented to the officials that those who raided her place had overlooked the movie. She knew that the officials could not help but examine and view all materials, including the movie. It is hard to say how many seeds were planted in hearts because of her wise, brave act.

In another incident a Chinese believer spent 24 years in prison because she would not change her mind about Jesus, regardless of the onslaught of re-education that was being thrust upon her. In one incident this woman was required to move a big rock by herself. While standing on the rock, she cried out to the Lord for His help to roll it back to its original place. Her prayer was answered and as a result many came to the saving knowledge of the Lord.

The final story involves a couple who were leaders of a large number of house churches in their area. One night the Red Guards kicked down their front door, tied both of them up, and shaved their heads bald. As they pointed their rifles at them, they demanded that they tell them where they were hiding the Bibles, who their co-workers were, and where they held meetings.

They refused to answer their questions. The guards turned their frustration on the house and begin to destroy the family's possessions. The silence of the couple caused the Red Guards to finally interrogate their four children. However, these young soldiers of the cross would not deny Christ. Sadly, the guard turned their wrath on the oldest boy. They beat him so badly that the doctor later told the mother there was no hope for his recovery. The son's request was that he be buried in white, breaking with the tradition of black burial clothes. As he was about to depart this world, the young man whispered to his parents that Jesus had come to take him to heaven. He told them goodbye and peacefully took the hand of his Lord.

Both parents were incarcerated. During the mother's incarceration she was given many opportunities to share her faith with her interrogators and those in prison. After a month, she was allowed to return home to discover that God had answered her main prayer by providing for her remaining children. Her children shared how the almost empty rice container miraculously proved to be overflowing with rice each day of her absence.

The mother was even sentenced to death for her belief. They lined her up in front of a firing squad with others. When the rifles fired, everyone lay dead on the ground but her. That night she was brought in for interrogation, sentencing, and execution. They actually dragged her up by the hair. They tied a rope around her wrists behind her back and then brought the rope up tight around her neck. She was then hung tautly from above. Most people would not survive the ordeal, but she did and once again she shared the reality of her Lord.

Since she was bleeding all over from her ordeal, as well as internally, the prison doctor signed a document that she was in terminal illness and soon to die, and she was released. However, the next day she was back to preaching and visiting the house church leaders to encourage them.

As you notice the main stories surround women believers. In some of the Church, women are sometimes demoted as to their importance in the kingdom of God. According to Paul Estabrooks of the Open Doors International, women make up over 70% of China's church – both official and unofficial. They are imprisoned, tortured, and killed just like their counterparts. If they are left behind to take care of this family, they must keep the fires going under grave oppression.

The book (from which these stories were retained) is entitled, *Great Bible Women of China.* Estabrooks noted how Corrie ten Boom said, "When God has a task to be done, He calls a man...a **difficult** task, He calls a woman!" He went on to quote a Cuban pastor who stated that, "Lenin said that without women there would be no revolution. I say that without women there would be no church!"

The Bible tells us there is no male or female in the kingdom of God. In fact, those vessels considered weak must be honored or exalted to ensure the proper function of the whole Body. It is clear that God has, continues to, and will use women to further His kingdom.

And many women were there beholding afar off, which followed Jesus from Galilee, ministering unto him (Matthew 27:55).

- God never wastes anything in our lives. He uses our challenges to enlarge us to receive more; our wounds to make us more compassionate; our failures to make us more realistic, and our defeats to make us victorious. In other words, all the hard lessons from the past can be made into priceless treasures that strengthen us for each new day and challenge.

  -RJK

- You may kill us, but you can't hurt us.

  -Justin Martyr
  (GPQ, pg. 176)

- Sanctified afflictions are spiritual promotions.

  -Matthew Henry

- The tree that is deeply founded in its root is not moved by the onset of winds.

  -Cyprian
  (DCB, pg. 549)

- We are chosen as an afflicted people and not as a prosperous people: chosen not in the place, but in the furnace.

  -Charles Spurgeon
  (FCB, pg. 248)

- Naturally, most of us want to avoid the fires of tribulation. Our flesh desires the promises without the price; however, if the Spirit leads us, there will be fiery trials on the "sanctification road". May we follow where He leads in complete faith and trust.

  -RJK

- The suffering of adversity does not degrade you but exalts you; human tribulation teaches you, it does not destroy you.

  -Isidore of Seville
  (GPQ, pg. 16)

Behold, I have refined thee, but not with silver; I have chosen thee in the furnace of affliction (Isaiah 48:10).

- I will die for my God. I will die for my faith. It's the least I can do for Christ dying for me.

  -Cassie Bernall
  Columbine High School Martyr

- In Revelation 2:10, Jesus is telling the local Church of Smyrna that the devil will cast some into prison, but to not fear any of those things that are associated to persecution for His sake. There is a certain inward environment that must be present if one is to stand in such persecution. It is that of being poor in spirit. Jesus knew this body of believers' works, tribulation, and poverty. The works showed that they had been purged. The tribulation revealed that they had been prepared. And, the poverty showed that the tribulation had succeeded in establishing a healthy inward environment that would enable them to stand in persecution.

-RJK

Blessed are they which are persecuted for righteousness' sake: for theirs is the kingdom of heaven (Matthew 5:10).

- There is no riding to heaven in a chariot; the rough way must be trodden; mountains must be climbed, rivers must be forded, dragons must be fought, giants must be slain, difficulties must be overcome, and great trials must be borne.

  -Anonymous

- When the threshing floor brings out the grain, the strong and robust grains ignore the winds, while the empty chaff is carried away by the blast that falls upon it.

  -Cyprian
  (DCB, pg. 549)

- Those who complain that they make no progress in the life of prayer because they "cannot meditate" should examine, not their capacity for meditation, but their capacity for suffering and love. For there is a hard and costly element, a deep seriousness, a crucial choice, in all genuine religion.

  -Evelyn Underhill

Yea, and all that will live godly in Christ Jesus shall suffer persecution (2 Timothy 3:12).

- We exaggerate all our sufferings by our cowardice. They are great, it is true, but they are magnified by fear. The way to lessen them is to abandon ourselves courageously into the hands of God. We must suffer, but the aim of our pain is to purify our souls, and make us worthy of Him.

  -Fenelon
  (TWG, pg. 98)

- Above all, we ought to endure everything for God's sake so that He may also endure us.

-Ignatius

- The martyrs were bound, imprisoned, scourged, racked, burnt, rent, butchered—and they multiplied.

-Augustine
(GPQ, pg. 50)

If we suffer, we shall also reign with him: if we deny him, he also will deny us (2 Timothy 2:12).

- My circumstances are such that I have no comfort of any kind but what I have in God.

-David Brainerd
(LDD, pg. 124)

******

The Message of Consecration

In his writings, an individual related how he had heard and read many great messages, but one of the messages that has stood out through the years was the one given by Dr. John G. Lake in 1920. It was delivered at an ordination service.

Dr. Lake started his message by talking about the Apostle Paul. The apostle was told up front that his ministry would not be an easy road to walk. He was not going to experience heavenly ecstasy or appear successful. He would end up having to endure some grave times of opposition and persecution. Lake went on to say that in the present atmosphere (of that day) Christians appeared to have lost that character of consecration, a virtue that God was trying to restore.

Since this message over one-hundred years ago, the concept of consecration seems to be even more so foreign. In my own observation I have noticed that Christians want to decide what altar they will be consecrated on and what kind of loss they will experience. If the loss does not allow them to maintain their present carnal lives, while being commended for such "nobility", they will usually have no part in the total abandonment called by consecration.

Lake went on in his message to ask if those present wanted to know why God at that particular time poured out His Spirit in South Africa. He continued to explain that there were 125 men who initially accepted the call to venture into a mission field that was far from home and foreign to them in every way. Since they were a young institution and relatively unknown, they found themselves in financially dire straights. The situation for these ministers and their families became desperate as the funds that came from other sources dwindled down to nothing. As a result, some ended up selling their clothes and certain pieces of furniture along with other articles in order to stay the course.

Dr. Lake did not want to take the responsibility of leaving these committed individuals in the dark about their real plight. He invited them to a conference. One night he was invited by the committee representing these ministers of the Gospel to leave the room for a minute so they could confer with one another in regard to the challenges that lay before them. When Lake stepped back into the room, the spokesman for the group told Dr. Lake that they had made a decision. They wanted him to serve the Lord's Supper. The spokesman then stated, "We are going back to the fields if we have to walk back. We are going back if we starve. We are going back if our wives die. We are going back if our children die. We are going back if we die ourselves. We have but one request. If we die, we want you to come and bury us."

Lake went on to say the next year he buried twelve men and sixteen wives and children. It was because of the sacrificial consecration of these committed servants that enabled the Lord to pour out His Spirit on South Africa. Dr. Lake stated that Jesus Christ put the spirit of martyrdom in the ministry. He went on to tell those at the ordination service that the missionaries who had followed him went without food and clothes. He spoke of the preacher that suffered from sun stroke and wandered away. He tracked him by the blood marks of his feet. Another missionary ventured into unknown territory without any shoes.

Because of our environment, the natural response is for our spirit to refuse to sacrifice, or consider the ways of death or suffering. Even though we are to walk as Jesus walked, we convince ourselves that He really would never require us to sacrifice in such measure. However, Jesus' example shows us differently. His sacrifice reveals that such a consecration is what will impact and move heaven.

There is a cost to know God and to prepare the environment for a real move of His Spirit. Much of the Church in America has been pampered by a materialistic lifestyle, dulled down by a worldly gospel, and made soft by fleshly wrong attitudes and mindsets. Although there are those who are calling for revival, it will never happen as long as the present environment of selfishness is left intact.

We need to let the example of Christ and the witness of those who have gone before us serve as an example as to the standard that must be raised on a personal level and a national level to change the present tides of wickedness. However, we must first count the cost. (TB, pgs. 232-238)

For even hereunto were ye called: because Christ also suffered for us, leaving us an example, that ye should follow his steps (1 Peter 2:21).

- What does it take to come into a place of abiding fellowship? The answer is suffering. Identification and fellowship in the kingdom of God entail suffering. It is suffering that makes us more pliable in the hands of God. Otherwise, our self-sufficiency will cause resistance to His ways. Our independence will try to find ways around His work. Our rebellion will oppose Him as we harden our hearts towards His truths and ways.

  -RJK

- There is a limit to affliction. God sends it and God removes it.

  -Charles Spurgeon

- Like gold reduced in the furnace, it (the faith) has only been made to shine the more under the storms of persecution.

  -Theonas of Alexandria
  (GPQ, pg. 50)

- *The secret formula of the saints:* When I am in the cellar of affliction, I look for the Lord's choicest wines.

  -Samuel Rutherford
  (PDC, pg. 79)

- Great hearts can only be made by great troubles. Great faith must have great trials"

  -Charles H. Spurgeon

Service

- A servant is not ashamed or humiliated by being regarded as an inferior; it is his place and work to serve others. The reason why we so often do not bless others is that we want to show that we are superior to them in grace or gifts, or at least their equals.

  -Andrew Murray

- Who we serve is a choice of the will. Who we follow is a choice of the heart. Who we honor is a choice of the mind.

  -RJK

Now therefore fear the LORD, and serve him in sincerity and in truth: and put away the gods which your fathers served on the other side of the flood, and in Egypt; and serve ye the LORD. And if it seem evil unto you to serve the LORD, choose you this day whom ye will serve; whether the gods which your father served that were on the other side of the flood or the gods of the Amorites, in whose land ye dwell: but as for me and my house, we will serve the LORD (Joshua 24:13-15).

- I see nothing else in the world that can yield any satisfaction besides living to God, pleasing Him, and doing His whole will.

  -David Brainerd

- All great leaders for God have fashioned their leadership in the wrestlings of their prayer closets.

  -E. M. Bounds
  (PP, pg. 7)

❖ Ministry for Christ is first ministry *to* Christ. It begins by sitting at His feet and learning who He is. It means sitting at His table and partaking of the daily food He gives. It means being faithful to Him, first, at all times so that as His life begins to be formed in us, then we in turn, are enabled to share that life with others.

-Jeannette Haley

❖ Oh that we may know our God—His power, His faithfulness, His immutable love—and so we may be ready to risk everything in His behalf.

-Charles Spurgeon

Not with eyeservice, as menpleasers; but as the servants of Christ, doing the will of God from the heart; With good will doing service, as to the Lord, and not to men (Ephesians 6:6-7).

❖ He is raised upon a high cross...Who was He? Painful it is to tell, more terrible not to tell.

-Melito of Sardis
(GPQ, pg. 70)

❖ God is going to give me a specific leading—not when I ask for it, but when I need it, and not until then.

-James Elliot
(SOA, pg. 127)

❖ Every Christian has one reason to approach God's Word, and that is to believe it. Every saint has one motivation for seeking God's will, and that is to obey. Every believer has one purpose for serving the Lord, and that is to bring glory to Him.

-RJK

Let your light so shine before men, that they may see your good works, and glorify your Father who is in heaven (Matthew 5:16).

- ❖ A good character is the best tombstone. Those who loved you and were helped by you will remember you when forget-me-nots have withered. Carve your name on hearts, not on marble.

  -C.H. Spurgeon

- ❖ The prayers of God's saints are a great factor, a supreme factor, in carrying forward God's work with ease and in time.

  -E. M. Bounds

******

Listen – hear the song!
It calls me to follow
walk
see.

-Maureen Human

And he hath put a new song in my mouth, even praise unto our God: many shall see it, and fear, and shall trust in the LORD (Psalm 40:3).

- ❖ Accustom yourself, in everything that happens, to recognize the hand and will of God.

  -Andrew Murray
  (LC, pg. 38)

- ❖ A pulpit without a prayer closet will always be a barren thing.

  -E. M. Bounds

- ❖ One wonders if it is not true that in the midst of the ail of jet engines, the crash of old orders, the mesmerism of materialism, the savage competition and worldly programs, we have lost an ear for the cry of millions dying "having no hope and without God in the world."

  -Leonard Ravenhill

- ❖ How can we expect non-Christians to awake if we ourselves are not awakened? How can 'fire" arise if we ourselves do not 'burn'?

How shall life be begotten if we ourselves are not truly filled with 'life'?

-Erich Sauer

Wherefore, he saith, Awake thou that sleepest, and arise from the dead, and Christ shall give thee light (Ephesians 5:14).

❖ The highest in glory will be he who was lowest in service, and most like the Master in His giving His life as a ransom.

-Andrew Murray

❖ God never has and He never will commit the weighty interests of His kingdom to people who do not make prayer a conspicuous and controlling factor in their lives.

-E. M. Bounds
(WOP, pg. 45)

❖ In the kingdom of God, greatness is measured by servitude. The greater the servant, the greater the leadership capacity such a person will have in God's kingdom. Those who become a minister to all will end up being the chief example of greatness to others.

-RJK

But Jesus called them unto him, and said, Ye know that the princes of the Gentiles exercise dominion over them, and they that are great exercise authority over them. But it shall not be so among you: but whosoever will be great among you, let him be your servant (Matthew 20:25-27).

❖ Solid, lasting missionary work is done on our knees."

-J.O. Fraser

❖ God doesn't call the equipped; He equips the called.

-Anonymous

- You will observe the difference between the crowds, who simply " followed" Christ, and Peter and the others who "gave up everything and followed."

-Origen

And every one that hath forsaken houses, or brethren, or sisters, or father, or mother, or wife, or children, or lands, for my name's sake, shall receive an hundredfold, and shall inherit everlasting life (Matthew 19:29).

The Day the Cows Came Home

In the high deserts of Arizona near Prescott is a small community called Hillside. It is surrounded by large cattle ranches. The center of this community is the community church. Jeannette and I have had the honor of ministering in this Christian place of worship. The pastor of the church is Galen Neshem. I must note that he was faithfully assisted in his many duties by his wife, Rodella. They were not only busy with seven children, but with their personal ministries. Rodella taught in a one-room class of young people from the first to the eighth grade.

Without a doubt Galen fits his surroundings for he is a cowboy preacher from the top of his cowboy hat to the bottom of his cowboy boots. In a sense he is a circuit preacher.

Although he also oversees a large cattle ranch, he has spent over three decades overseeing believers, not only in Hillside but in various small surrounding communities with names like Walnut Grove. At the time we ministered at the Hillside church, he took us to other fellowships. We got a small taste of how busy he was as he juggled many responsibilities on both the home front and being faithful to do the work of the kingdom of God. He once told me that his circuit as a pastor encompassed an eighty-mile radius.

On one occasion he shared a story with me that I have never forgotten. Granted, since I heard it over 30 years ago, my mind is a bit duller and the details a bit fudged, but the intent of it remains fresh and alive.

One day he received a call from a believer that needed ministry. He was about to ride out into the desert brushy countryside to find some lost strays. As he wrestled with what he needed to do, the Lord settled the matter. He told him if he would take care of His business, He would take care of his. With his spirit settled, he hurried off to see the struggling brother.

When he finally arrived home in the late afternoon, he saddled up his horse to locate the strays. As he was riding down the road, something caught his eye. Can you imagine what caught his attention? Ready to be gathered up, were the missing cattle.

It was clear that since Galen had done God's business, God was true to His word and took care of Galen business by bringing home the cows.

(Update: Since the first publication of this book ten years ago in 2013, Galen and Rodella celebrated their 62nd anniversary this year, 2023, and he recently retired, but neither one will ever let the grass grow under their feet. They may be a bit slower but they are ever busy celebrating the life and different families, both physical and spiritual that God has entrusted to them, along with the message of the cross that never grows old.)

And he said unto them, How is it that ye sought me? Wist ye not that I must be about my Father's business (Luke 2:49)?

The Issues of the Christian Life

- Every place and every time in which we entertain the idea of God is in reality sacred.

  -Clement of Alexandria

- The measure of a life, after all, is not its duration, but its donation.

  -Catherine Marshall
  (JMM, pg. 16)

- This life is a dressing room for eternity - THAT'S ALL IT IS!"

  -Leonard Ravenhill

- It is not the sty that makes the pig, but the pig that makes the sty.

  -Samuel Chadwick

- Running the Christian race is not based on speed, but endurance. It is a marathon that requires commitment and intense preparation. The course is hard and it spans the duration of the Christian journey through the present age.

  -RJK

- Christianity began as a personal relationship with Jesus Christ. When it went to Athens, it became a philosophy. When it went to Rome, it became an organization. When it went to Europe, it became a culture. When it came to America, it became a business.

  -Steve Quayle video

Give not that which is holy unto the dogs, neither cast ye your pearls before swine, lest they trample them under their feet, and turn again and rend you (Matthew 7:6).

❖ Unless we have WITHIN us that which is ABOVE us, we will eventually yield to that which is AMONG us.

-Unknown

******

A Simple Truth

What does the Christian life really look like? Is it represented by putting the best foot forward when seen by others, wearing a plastic smile in church, or displaying an exuberant show of love towards those who are part of the cliquish crowd?

I remember hearing a story about a church back east where the people played at being the church, but did not appear to possess any real love or concern for souls. A young man came to church one day. He sat off by himself, while the rest of the people greeted each other in the same fashion they always did. Since the young man was not part of the crowd, he was ignored. That night the lone young man came to church once again. Like the morning service, he was ignored. While business was being conducted as usual during the church service, the young man stood up in his lonely pew, put a gun to his head and shot himself.

This story greatly impacted me. I could not help but wonder if the gunshot, blood, and death of a young man were enough to actually wake some of these people out of their indifferent, loveless, lifeless, religious state of foolish vanity. How many lost souls are falling through the cracks as we carry on our social, surface business in our churches? How many of these poor individuals are allowed to commit spiritual suicide because Christians lack any real vision, concern, or compassion towards the lost? How many have failed to come to an understanding that all who considered themselves to be Christians have all been commissioned to preach the Gospel and make disciples of Christ? How many understand that the Christian life is not some type of "religious cloak" you put on every Sunday and discard during the rest of the week as a means to fit into the world? Either individuals are being conformed to the world's indifference to the matters of eternity and the carnal way of thinking, or they are being conformed by the life of Christ in them, thereby, expressing His attitude and life.

When my co-laborer, Jeannette was in junior high school, she remembers a sign that hung in her classroom. It read, "I am what I am when I am not being watched." The truth is that the essence of people's character is not measured by the type of show they can put on when the different lights of the world are upon them; rather true character is revealed by the type of person they are behind closed doors. Anyone can be a good actor for a period of time, but such an individual cannot continue to be something he or she is not when the stage lights of the world have become dimmed by darkness. It is for this reason the real measure of a person's character will be revealed behind closed doors. How does he or she treat those who live with him or her? How do these individuals respond to crises? How prideful and spoiled are they when it comes to demanding their way?

Even though we can act a part for a while, we cannot be someone we are not when no one is really watching. Our best is always for the limelight, while our worst is hidden by the darkness of independence, ignorance, and delusion. In such cases our best is nothing more than a flash in the pan, and our worst marks the essence of our real character.

The Bible is clear that the greatest revealer of our true character is how we treat the stranger, the needy, the unacceptable, and rejected among us. True sustaining character possesses a genuine concern for those who are poor in spirit. It cannot ignore those who sit at a distance out of fear, hide in the shadows of insecurity, and seem aloof in an attitude of indifference or rebellion. Like the God who inspired it, that which is eternal and genuine can do no less than reach out with the compassionate, sacrificial love of heaven, knowing full well that it might taste the thorns of mockery, the indifference of hatred, the rejection of anger, and the despair of sorrow. Clearly, when Jesus embraced the cross, it was for the sole purpose of reaching poor lost souls with the glorious hope of heaven.

As believers, can we be any less than excellent in our commitment towards others and any less sacrificial in our lives before the Lord than He was on the cross? Jesus made it clear that the one Christian virtue that will distinguish us as part of His Church is genuine love.

Pure religion and undefiled before God and the Father is this: to visit the fatherless and widows in their affliction, and to keep oneself unspotted from the world (James 1:27).

- John Wesley's blueprint for living was:

  Do All the Good You Can,
  By all the Means You Can
  In All the Ways You Can
  In All the Places You Can,
  At All the Times You Can.
  To All the People You Can,
  As long as Ever You Can!

- Small deeds done are better than great deeds planned.

  -Peter Marshall

- Communion with God is the life of religion. It is but a dead thing without it . . . What the body is without the soul, and matter without form, that is religion, where men find no influence from heaven upon their hearts, and have no communion with God.

  -Matthew Barker
  Puritan Minister
  (PDC, pg. 235)

- Reading makes a full man, prayer a holy man, temptation an experienced man.

  -John Trapp

- The will of God is always a bigger thing than we bargain for.

  -James Elliot

******

Out of This Life

Out of this life I shall never take
    Things of silver and gold I make.
All that I cherish and hoard away
    After I leave, on this earth must stay.

Tho' I have toiled for a painting rare
    To hang on the wall, I must leave it there.
Though I called it mine, and boast its worth,
    I must give it up when I leave this earth.

All that I gather, and all that I keep,
    I must leave behind when I fall asleep.
And I often wonder what I shall own
    In that other life, when I pass alone.

What shall they find, and what
    Shall they see, in the soul that
Answers the call for me?

Shall the Great Judge learn,
    When my task is through
That my spirit has gained some riches, too?
    Or shall, at least, it be mine to find
That all I'd worked for I'd left behind?

-Author Unknown

- Christianity is a life. This life is the life of Christ in us. His life is eternal. Therefore, the one aspect of His life is that it is ongoing. It is meant to change, enlarge, and bring purpose to every believer. Life that remains stagnant in a believer becomes unbearable. Life that lacks challenge becomes aimless. Life that is never enlarged by learning the lessons of life becomes spiritually small and dull. Life that is not disciplined becomes useless. Clearly, the life of Christ must be experienced and lived out in every area of our lives.

It is meant to make us into new creations that become living expressions of our Lord and Savior.

-RJK

I am crucified with Christ: nevertheless I live; yet not I but Christ liveth in me: and the life which I now live in the flesh I live by the faith of the Son of God, who loved me, and gave himself for me (Galatians 2:20).

- We do not speak great things—we live them.

  -Mark Minucius Felix
  (DCB, pg. 548)

- Man proposes, but God disposes.

  -Peter Marshall
  (JMM, pg. 166)

- Our very life must be held not as a selfish possession but as a sacred trust.

  -A.B. Simpson

- Don't plan without God. God seems to have a delightful way of upsetting the plans we have made, when we have not taken Him into account.

  -Oswald Chambers

- A man says to me, "Can you explain the seven trumpets of the Revelation?" No, but I can blow one in your ear, and warn you to escape from the wrath to come.

  -C.H. Spurgeon

And to wait for his Son from heaven, whom he raised from the dead, even Jesus, which delivered us from the wrath to come (1 Thessalonians 1:10).

******

God's Balance

When we think of life in light of God, we think of a balance. In weighing matters in light of facing God, it is natural for man to erect a balance where his bad is weighed against what he considers to be good. He recognizes that there are "bad" things he has done because he has a moral sense as to what is right and what is wrong. If his moral sense has been seared, he is left with nothing more than the bitter taste of the fruit that his wrong ways have produced.

However, does God use the same type of balance when it comes to weighing the brevity of man's life? In Daniel 5, we get a glimpse of God's balance. When King Belshazzar's contemptible actions caused God to reveal His balance to the king, it was clear that Belshazzar's actions brought an end to his kingdom. But what was made clear from God's balance, was what was being weighed in the balance, which was not the king's deeds, works, or actions, but his very person, the summation of the type of life resonating in him.

The balance between good and bad is based on the world's measurement, but when it comes to God, His balance will pit His holy Law against the type of life in us. It is obvious that God's perception of "good" and man's perception of it are far apart.

When it comes to these two balances, it is clear that in people's minds they perceive that if they do enough "good" things, their deeds will outweigh their bad actions and God will surely give them a pass. The Bible is clear that God does not weigh our good with our bad. The reason is because according to Romans 7:18, there is no "good" thing in the flesh and Isaiah 64:6 tells us our best is considered filthy rags.

It is for this reason that God weighs the type of life in us against His holy, perfect Law. Since the Law is unable to justify a person in an unacceptable state of sin, it can only find each of us guilty of breaking it. The truth is we have all broken God's Law in some way. Our selfish disposition will justify us when trespassing into forbidden areas of the Law, while our wrong attitudes will pervert its holy intent, and our defiant actions will transgress it.

John 3:3 and 5 tells us we must be born again to enter the kingdom of God. Upon the new birth we receive a new heart and spirit. The new heart possesses the life of Christ, while the new spirit ensures that the new life is worked in, through, and out of us. Since Christ fulfilled the Law, He satisfied the judgment of death that rested upon all of us. As Romans 10:4 states that Jesus is the end of the Law for righteousness to everyone who believes.

When we received Jesus, Colossians 3:3 tells us that we became hid in Him. Since we are hid in Him, we know according to Ephesians 2:6 that we are also positionally seated in high places with Him. According to Romans 8:2, we have been placed under a more excellent Law, the Law of the Spirit of life in Christ Jesus.

When God weighs us as believers in the balance, the life that is weighed against His Law is the life of Jesus in us. In Him the fullness of wisdom, righteousness, sanctification, and redemption resonates in and through us. Since Jesus satisfied the Law, His life in us serves as the essence of righteousness and completes the intent of the Law. The result is we stand justified before God, rather than condemned. Clearly, the life of Jesus must be present in a person for him or her to avoid facing the wrath of God against what His Law deems as ungodliness and unrighteousness on the part of unregenerate and rebellious man.

TEKEL; Thou are weighed in the balances, and art found wanting (Daniel 5:27).

❖ There is something infinitely better than doing a great thing for God, and the infinitely better thing is to be where God wants us to be, to do what God wants us to do, and to have no will apart from His.

-G. Campbell Morgan

❖ Wherever you are, be all there. Live to the hilt of every situation you believe to be the will of God...Let not our longing slay the appetite of our living.

-Jim Elliot

❖ God always has His remnant of people who will never bow their knees to the Baals of their ages. They may be hidden away by the darkness of slavery and poverty, but their hearts remain steadfast towards God even though they live in insane times. Like Gideon, they may be threshing behind the winepress, but their spiritual search always lead them back to the reality of the one true God. In silence they may have to cleave to the past victories of God, ponder the possibilities of their Creator in regard to the present, and trust that regardless of the circumstances, in the end the Lord will ultimately be exalted as the only true God of heaven and earth.

-RJK

❖ What I have seen in the past 10 years of traveling - performing at a church one day and a casino the next - is that a lot of people in the church want to be entertained, and people in casinos want to be ministered to. That's hard to understand, but I see a hunger in the world that I don't see in the church.

-Ricky Shaggs
Musician

❖ One of the cardinal rules of the spiritual life is that we are to live in the present moment.

-Fenelon

❖ Life is to be measured by action, not by time; a man may die old at thirty, and young at eighty; nay, the one lives after death, and the other perished before he died.

-Thomas Fuller
(PDC, pg. 369)

❖ It is in the text of James 4:13-15 that we are reminded that our lives are a vapor in light of eternity. We think we are so big, but consider the universe. We think we are strong, but face the power of rushing water or a strong wind, and see how strong we can be against such elements. We think we are so smart, but our minds cannot grasp eternity. It is because of such foolish conclusions about personal strength that many walk in unbelief towards God.

-RJK

Like as a father pitieth his children, so the LORD pitieth them that fear him. For he knoweth our frame; he remembereth that we are dust. As for man, his days are like grass: as a flower of the field, so he flourisheth. For the wind passeth over it, and it is gone; and the place thereof shall know it no more (Psalm 103:13-16).

- Men are not born Christians but become such.

  -Tertullian
  (GPQ, pg. 45)

- If you don't plan to live the Christian life totally committed to knowing your God and to walk in obedience to Him, then don't begin; for this is what Christianity is all about. It is a change of citizenship, a change of governments, a change of allegiance. If you have no intention of letting Christ rule your life, then forget Christianity; it's not for you.

  -K. Arthur

- We shall have all eternity in which to celebrate our victories, but we have only one swift hour before the sunset in which to win them.

  -Robert Moffat

- The more of heaven there is in our lives, the less of earth we shall covet.

  -Charles Spurgeon

- I would say, first of all, that this blessed life must not be looked upon in any sense as an attainment, but as an obtainment. We cannot earn it, we cannot climb up to it, we cannot win it; we can do nothing but ask for it and receive it. It is the gift of God in Christ Jesus.

  -Hannah Whitall Smith

- The world is enough to busy us, but not fill us.

  -Thomas Watson

- Sometimes we are so busy chasing the "big" things that we fail Christ in the small, everyday things.

  -Jeannette Haley

- The Christian ideal has not been tried and found wanting. It has been found difficult and left untried."

  -G. K. Chesterton

- Much of the Christian life is comprised of wilderness. It appears as if the person is not getting anywhere in life. However, to God, it is not the distance one travels as much as the preparation one gives way to in order to be victorious.

  -RJK

Being confident of this very thing, that he which hath begun a good work in you will perform it until the day of Jesus Christ (Philippians 1:6).

- All we have acquired by natural birth from Adam is to be sold, if we are to possess the pearl of great price.

  -Andrew Murray

- Only when I am commanded to deny Him, will I not obey.

  -Tatian
  (GPQ, pg. 191)

- In our initial ill-tempered, unregenerate state, we all possess the same attitude as Lucifer displayed in Isaiah 14:12-15. I *WILL* control my reality, my world, and my life. I *WILL* ascend in my arrogance in the matters concerning life. I *WILL* exalt my ways in regards to life. I *WILL* sit on the throne, ruling over the ways of life. I *WILL* ascend above the challenges of life, and in the end, I *WILL* be like the Most High in the matters of life.

  -RJK

For God doth know that in the day ye eat thereof, then your eyes shall be opened, and ye shall be as gods, knowing good and evil (Genesis 3:5).

- I have learned, in a measure that all good things, relating both to time and eternity, comes from God.

-David Brainerd
(LDD, 139)

******

The Balm in Gilead
is green and gentle
to the breeze.
A dry desert-hot and thirsty
opens up to take in seas.

A thorn with crimson
Stain has been made white
by that which what was bought
with a price.

Redeem the time
For what was sent
from above—
A pearl of great price.

Wisdom—in all her glory
Cannot compare with a heart
That has been cleansed,
Restructured piece by piece
by the Master's hand.

-Maureen Human

- I see with greater and greater clearness that consistent Christianity is the easiest Christianity to defend.

-J. Gresham Machen

❖ People who do not know the Lord ask why in the world we waste our lives as missionaries. They forget that they too are expending their lives ... and when the bubble has burst, they will have nothing of eternal significance to show for the years they have wasted.

-Nate Saint
Missionary pilot and martyr

Redeeming the time, because the days are evil. Wherefore be ye not unwise, but understanding what the will of the Lord is (Ephesians 5:16-17).

❖ How do we learn to cherish life? We must learn to value that which truly brings substance to it. When life holds no value or purpose, it is because we value that which holds no real significance in regard to the matters of eternity.

-RJK

For where your treasure is, there will your heart be also (Matthew 6:21).

❖ He that seems righteous toward men, and is irreligious toward God, is but an honest heathen; and he that seems religious toward God, and is unrighteous toward men, is but a fake Christian.

-George Swinnock
(PDC, pg. 346)

❖ Prayer is the mainspring of life, we pray as we live, we live as we pray.

-E. M. Bounds
(WOP, pg. 58)

❖ Therefore the Lord blesses His habitation. It may be a humble cottage or a lordly mansion, but the Lord's blessing comes because of the character of the inhabitant and not because of the size of the dwelling.

-Charles Spurgeon

- Salvation of our souls lies at the core of all spiritual matters and truths. Serve whom you will, but if it is not the true God of heaven, you remain lost to Him. Worship who you will, but if it is not the God of the Bible, it will all be in vain. Dance around your religious altars with penance, declarations, flags, and outward show of piousness, but if such worship has not been consecrated in your heart to the only God of heaven, all such activities will be considered perverted, foreign, and strange to Him. Do all the religious works you can, but if they are not inspired or born out of genuine faith towards the true God of heaven, such works will be considered reprobate.

  -RJK

- We are exhorted to lay down our own life that His life may be lived in us; we are asked to have no interests but His interests, to share His riches, to enter into His joys, to partake of His sorrows, to manifest His likeness, to have the same mind as He had, to think and feel and act and walk as He did.

  -Hannah Whitall Smith

- You know what abiding in Him is? It is to consent with our whole souls to His being in our lives, to depend on Him to inspire us in all that goes to make up life, and then to absolutely give up everything so that He may rule and work in us...He Himself enables us to maintain that perfect surrender, in which He is freed to do all His will.

  -Andrew Murray

If a man abide not in me, he is cast forth as a branch, and is withered; and men gather them, and cast them into the fire, and they are burned (John 15:6).

******

Facing Mortality

We all must face our mortality. We do not know how long we have in this world. We are all like a flower whose beauty will fade in time and grass that will wither with the change of seasons. It is hard for man to face his own mortality. After all, man is meant to live forever, but not in his present state. The corruptible must give way to the incorruptible.

A man who faced his mortality off and on up to the ripe "old" age of 29 when he finally succumbed to the claims of death upon his corruptible body, was missionary David Brainerd. He summarized his attitude towards his life before God with this statement, "I hardly ever so longed to live to God and to be altogether devoted to Him. I wanted to wear out my life in His service, and for His glory. "

Brainerd's missionary work among the Native Americans in the 1700s reveals how God takes weak vessels and does mighty works through them. The incredible and miraculous occurred as God translated many sin-laden people from the kingdom of darkness into the kingdom of His dear Son during Brainerd work among these precious souls.

Brainerd had consumption that eventually opened the door to the glory of the promise of his own heavenly immortality. We can follow Brainerd's challenging experiences, the great travailing for souls, and the blissful joy of seeing souls saved in his journals. During those times he was facing his mortality as the disease was wrecking havoc on his body, he records his thoughts and prayers. I like to share some of these entries with you.

On September 27th, he felt that he would not recover from his illness, but he chose to trust the faithful providence of God He stated that with, "great composure he could look death in the face." David went on to make this declaration, "Oh, how blessed it is, to be habitually prepared for death! The Lord grant that I may be actually ready also!"

In David's October 2nd entry, he talked about how his soul was set on the Lord, and how he longed to be with him. He wrote about his concern for eternity and his desire was to see God's kingdom come to the world. He wanted people to love the Lord. His request was simple, "Oh, come, Lord Jesus, come quickly! Amen."

Brainerd was engaged to be married to Jonathan Edwards' daughter, Jerusha. She was the one who chiefly attended him during the dark times of his illness. On the morning of October 4th he penned these words, "Dear Jerusha, are you willing to part with me? I am quite willing to part with you. Though, if I had thought I should not see you and be happy with you in another world, I could not bear to part with you. But we shall spend a happy eternity together." (It was noted by Edwards that it pleased a holy and sovereign God to take away his dear child, Jerusha by death following a short illness, on the fourteenth of February the following year of Brainerd's departure, in the eighteenth year of her age.)

Evening of October 4th: In the evening, as one came into the room with a Bible in her hand, Brainerd expressed himself thus: "Oh, that dear Book! That lovely Book! I shall soon see it opened! The mysteries that are in it, and the mysteries of God's providence, will be all unfolded." His Lord received David Brainerd into glory on October 9, 1747. One cannot help but realize that it was indeed a glorious exit for this saint as he was finally welcomed home by the loving arms of His Lord. (LDD, pgs.373-374)

Precious in the sight of the LORD is the death of his saints (Psalm 116:15).

❖ Be as useful and profitable as you can, for when you are brought to death your work will be over. Be careful to be making preparations for it. We live to learn to die. Our business is not to get riches, honours, or pleasures, but that we may depart in peace with God. Every corpse is a sermon; every tomb a teacher; every funeral an oration—to persuade you to learn to die.

-Mr. Doolittle
Matthew Henry's Commentary

❖ For Christians to forget the Lord means that they will give way to the world as they get caught up with religious activities, rather than the Person of Jesus. They become pious rather than obedient, self-righteous rather than humble, arrogant rather than meek, and superior rather than needy. In such a state, it is clear that these individuals have ultimately forgotten that the blood of Jesus is what purged them from their sin.

-RJK

For if these things be in you, and abound, they make you that ye shall neither be barren nor unfruitful in the knowledge of our Lord Jesus Christ. But he that lacketh these things is blind, and cannot see afar off, and hath forgotten that he was purged from his old sins (2 Peter 1:8-9).

❖ It is good to feel how weak we are, and to learn by experience that emotional fervor comes and goes.

-Fenelon
(TWG, pg. 123)

❖ God's life is like a gate, door, or veil. These entryways point to Jesus' redemption as the gate, His life as the door, and the place of communion and rest as the veil. Each of these entrances represents a greater revelation of the life we can have in our Lord.

-RJK

❖ Christ lived on earth so that He might show forth the image of God in His life. He lives in heaven so that we may show forth the image of God in our lives.

-Andrew Murray

❖ You must understand where you have been before you can determine where you need to venture.

-RJK

- Why is a person who does not completely trust in Christ called a Christian? The name of Pharisee is more fitting.

-Cyprian
(DCB, pg. 548)

- The satisfying Christian life is not found in the concept that I will be spared from hell, but in the confidence that I will be able to stand before my Lord, knowing that I have not brought any reproach or shame upon Him, His Name, or His kingdom.

-RJK

Prayer

- Prayer does not fit us for the greater works; prayer is the greater work.

  -Oswald Chambers

- Man has personal relations with God, and prayer is the divinely appointed means by which man comes into direct connection with God.

  -E. M. Bounds

- Prayer does not condition God; prayer conditions us. Prayer does not win God to our view; it reveals God's view to us. Prayer is not merit, so that by withdrawing from the world we of necessity gain special favors of God. Prayer is not purchasing things from God. If you ask why we emphasize prayer so much and so often, we reply, "Because Jesus did so."

  -Leonard Ravenhill
  (RPR, pg. 124)

- Historically, the church Jesus said He would build was born in a prayer-meeting, and its life can only be maintained in the same atmosphere.

  -Herbert Lockyer
  (MP, pg. 175)

- When we become too glib in prayer, we are most surely talking to ourselves.

  - A. W. Tozer

- Is prayer your steering wheel or your spare tire?

  -Corrie Ten Boom

Ye ask, and receive not, because ye ask amiss, that ye may consume it upon your lusts (James 4:3).

******

The Secret

I met God in the morning,
When my day was at its best,
And His presence came like sunrise,
Like a glory in my breast.
All day long the Presence lingered,
All day long He stayed with me,
And we sailed in perfect calmness
O'er a very troubled-sea.
So I think I know the secret,
Learned from many a troubled way:
You must see Him in the morning
If you want Him through the day.

On the back of the business card
of Ned Christie

O God, thou art my God; early will I seek thee: my soul thirsteth for thee, my flesh longeth for thee in a dry and thirsty land, where no water is; To see thy power and thy glory, so as I have seen thee in the sanctuary (Psalm 63:1-2).

******

Teach Us to Pray

One of the struggles I have had in my spiritual life surrounds prayer. I am sure this struggle is not unusual for other believers. After all, greatness in the kingdom of God seems to be attached to an effective prayer life. The fact that even the disciples asked Jesus to teach them to pray is a good example that no matter how religious we might think we are, we cannot assume that we know how to effectively pray.

When we consider the prayer life of others, an interesting picture emerges. It is said of Jonathan Edwards that he spent hours each day in prayer and studying the Bible. We have the example of George Mueller who simply spoke to God as if He was sitting at a table sipping tea with Him.

There was also A. W. Tozer. It was said of him that when he prayed, people felt as if God was right at his elbow. Tozer simply would shut out everything and everyone and focus on God. He would in essence practice daily the presence of God.

I learned of a particular saintly woman known for her prayer life. She made a living washing the clothes of others. While she washed the clothes, the washtub became her altar as her prayers went heavenward about the matters of life, people, and the world. It was said of her prayers that they clearly changed the dynamics of situations.

What do we need to understand about effective prayer? According to a book entitled, *Prayer Warriors*, there is no real secret to a successful prayer life that has not been unveiled in Scripture and example. In the case of the woman known as Holy Ann, the secret to her prayer life was that she possessed a child-like faith. Before she met Christ, Ann was ignorant and unteachable. She had a restless spirit and her temper would get the best of her. However, when God got a hold of her, she learned how to get a hold of God. She was a clear slate still untainted by worldly deduction and education. As a result, her unfeigned faith became a place of communion. She could not imagine in her child-like faith God not hearing or answering prayers that were pure in intent and sensitive to His heart and ways. No detail was to small or great. If there was a concern, then it had to be presented to the Lord. Granted, she developed this prayer life through adversity, but such adversity refined her inward disposition to maintain purity and simplicity in her prayer life. Her example teaches us that the inward disposition must possess a sincere, simple nature in order to pray with expectation.

There was the plumber, Thomas Haire who knew how to get a hold of God. However, his approach was that of a soldier. He knew there was a battle raging between unseen kingdoms, and that nothing would be accomplished unless the enemy was stopped in his tracks. It was clear that when the plumber went into prayer it was to thwart the advancement of the enemy. He understood that unless the enemy was put at bay, there could be no expectation of victory. The plumber teaches that the ordinary man can become extraordinary when prayer is used to further the kingdom of God. However, this extraordinary quality requires a person to understand his or her mission and the authority he or she has to carry it out in everyday living. To thwart the kingdom of Satan requires personal discipline that is borne out of travailing and intercession in the secret chambers of prayer.

Another prayer warrior was a man by the name of Edward Drury Whiteside. He was from Pittsburg and had a reputation of being a "Praying Man." He ministered in slums and prisons for much of his life. A year before this man died he said, "I desire to live that I may pray. I do not want to go to heaven yet. I want to stay a while longer to pray." Why was this man enthusiastic about prayer? It is because he knew prayer worked. It got things accomplished that no government, group of people, or the progressive means of the world could do. After all, God is the only real majority that counts in a matter. He is the only one who is capable of doing the impossible. This man knew that what counted to God were souls. He knew the Lord understood needs had to be met, hearts healed, and souls made whole to further His glorious kingdom.

Whiteside did nothing unless it was bathed in prayer. This included reading the Bible. He knew that to pray without the study of God's Word creates fanatics; and to study the Word intellectually and without much prayer creates cold theologians, likely to preach the Word in the killing letter and without the life-giving Spirit.

As you can see, each person had a different prayer life and focus. Their examples teach us that we must develop our own prayer lives. We must construct our own places where we can become shut in with our Lord, even when we are in public. Can you imagine how powerful the Church would be if each member effectively developed his or her own prayer life? If the Church indeed became a praying Church, great inroads would be made in the great harvest field of humanity.

For me, I discovered that my prayer life was a matter of just speaking to the Lord as I would a friend, a spouse, a father, and Lord. As my friend there is nothing I would not share with Him. As my spouse, there is no decision I would not make without Him. As my Father, I would always first seek His guidance and wisdom. As my Lord, I would do nothing unless instructed to do so.

The question is, have you developed your own prayer life? Do not compare yourself with others; rather, consider their example and come to terms with the type of discipline God desires to develop in you, as well as your mission in regard to His kingdom. An effective prayer life is a disciplined life. It is a point of identification. Even though Haire was involved with Evangelist Leonard Ravenhill and A. W. Tozer, and Whiteside was associated with conducting successful annual Bible and missionary conventions in Carnegie Music Hall, each of these saints' power rested in the fact that they knew God. Their relationship with God set them apart to be part of the move and work of God.

******

❖ Have you noticed how much praying for revival has been going on of late - and how little revival has resulted? I believe the problem is that we have been trying to substitute praying for obeying, and it simply will not work. To pray for revival while ignoring the plain precept laid down in Scripture is to waste a lot of words and get nothing for our trouble. Prayer will become effective when we stop using it as a substitute for obedience.

-A.W. Tozer

❖ We sabotage much of our praying by disobedience.

-Leonard Ravenhill
(RPR, pg. 158)

❖ Prayer, like everything else in God's universe, is not accidental in its way of working. It is based on laws—spiritual laws—in their field just as constant and inexorable and fixed as their companions in the natural realm.

-Peter Marshall
(JMM, pg. 62)

❖ The prayer life in which there are no miracles may be the greatest miracle of all.

-Samuel Chadwick

❖ Today, we are living in desperate times, Yet, the Church is not desperate before God in prayer.

-Chuck Smith

Confess your faults one to another, and pray one for another, that ye may be healed. The effectual, fervent prayer of a righteous man availeth much (James 5:16).

❖ Nothing is done well without prayer for the simple reason that it leaves God out of the work. It is so easy to be seduced by the good to the neglect of the best, until both the good and the best perish.

-E. M. Bounds

❖ Temptation and self-interest will dehumanize you. In theory we abhor lustful thoughts, but once temptation enters our heart, all contrary reasonings are overcome and silenced. If we do not abide in prayer, we will abide in temptation. Let this be one aspect of our daily intercession. "God, preserve my soul, and keep my heart and all its ways so that I will not be entangled".

-John Owen
(ST, pg. 111)

And lead us not into temptation, but deliver us from evil: For thine is the kingdom, and the power, and the glory, for ever. Amen (Matthew 6:13).

❖ (In regard to those praying saints that knew how to reach the throne of God) Most of us are but sparrows in prayer and flutter no higher than the lowest branches; but these "eagle" men soar into the heavenlies.

-Leonard Ravenhill

- One poor soul entered the school of prayer after his arrival in hell. He asked for relief from his agony; it was refused. He asked that a beggar warn his brothers; he was turned down. He was praying to Abraham, a man; he could not locate God. He dared not ask to get out; he plainly knew that he was beyond all hope. Prayerless on earth, unanswered in hell, he suffers on as the man who tried to learn to pray too late.

  -Cameron V. Thompson
  The Master Secrets of Prayer

- Let your whole heart be set upon the living God as the teacher when you enter your prayer closet.

  -Andrew Murray

- A holy life would not be so difficult and rare if our praying were not so brief, cold, and superficial.

  -E. M. Bounds

- It has been said, "Tears without prayers are vain." In a time of calamity it might be right to say, "Prayers without tears are vain." In a time of war we have heard people pray with more concern about their skins than their sins.

  -Leonard Ravenhill
  (RPR, pg. 118)

If I regard iniquity in my heart, the Lord will not hear me (Psalm 66:18).

- We need a Heaven-sent revival, a burning fire from on high,
  A purifying passion and a forsaking of our stubborn pride.
  We need a vision of eternity, of Hell and the Judgement Day,
  A fervent love for our Savior, that will gladly serve and obey.
  We need a Pentecostal purging and a breaking deep within,
  A vision of God Almighty and a river of tears for our nation's sin.
  We need a Heaven-sent revival, a burning fire set ablaze.
  Yet, we'll never see such glory, until the Church begins to pray.

  -David Smithers

- I have generally found that the more I do in secret prayer the more I have delighted to do, and have enjoyed more of a spirit of prayer; and frequently have found the contrary, when with journeying or otherwise I have been much deprived of retirement.

  -David Brainerd
  (LDD, pg. 126)

- A pulpit without a prayer closet will always be a barren thing.

  -E. M. Bounds

- Praying in secret means prevailing in public.

  -Leonard Ravenhill

- Prayer is not about changing the circumstances, but gaining the strength and confidence to carry on in spite of them.

  -RJK

- The true God is the God who answers by fire. And the true man of God is he who knows how to call down the fire because he has power with the God of heaven.

  -Andrew Murray
  (DEG, pg. 32)

Hear me, O LORD, hear me, that this people may know that thou art the LORD God, and that thou hast turned their heart back again. Then the fire of the LORD fell, and consumed the burnt sacrifice, and the wood, and the stones, and the dust, and licked up the water that was in the trench (1 Kings 18:37-38).

- The men and women of spiritual character and strength always valued prayer.

  -E. M. Bounds
  (WOP, pg. 48)

- Christlike praying in secret will be the secret of Christlike living in public.

  -Andrew Murray
  (LC, pg. 127)

- So often we pray after we have fallen into the den of lions. Many times had we known the mind of the Spirit, that the den needs not have been ours. Because we are not yearning in prayer and burning with compassion, men are not turning to God. But men must turn or burn. We must weep or "sleep," for we cannot do both.

  -Leonard Ravenhill
  (RPR, pg. 130)

- All God's saints came to their sainthood by way of prayer.

  -E. M. Bounds
  (WOP, pg. 105)

- A prayerful, humble spirit is the spirit to which God will speak.

  -RJK

- Work as if everything depended upon your work, and pray as if everything depended upon your prayer.

  -William Booth

Praying always with all prayer and supplication in the Spirit, and watching thereunto with all perseverance and supplication for all saints (Ephesians 6:18).

- God made prayer one of the granite forces upon which His world movements would be based.

  -E. M. Bounds

- Courage is fear prayed for.

  -Unknown

- How hard is it sometimes to get leave of hearts to seek God! Jesus Christ went more willingly to the cross than we do to the throne of grace.

  -Thomas Watson

And he spake a parable unto them to this end, that men ought always to pray, and not to faint (Luke 18:1).

❖ Even the fishes of the great deep are subject to the law of prayer.

-E. M. Bounds

❖ I write here by constraint, for my spirit is sore, my heart sick at the slothfulness with which we tarry in prayer. My head hangs low that Communists will give more for their dying cause than we will give for the living Christ.

-Leonard Ravenhill

And, behold, I send the promise of my Father upon you: but tarry ye in the city of Jerusalem, until ye be endued with power from on high (Luke 24:49).

❖ When alone with God, be alone with Him.

-Samuel Chadwick

❖ When God is lifted up in sincere praise, man is lifted spiritually and emotionally above the circumstances.

-RJK

Pray without ceasing. In everything give thanks: for this is the will of God in Christ Jesus concerning you (1 Thessalonians 5:17-18).

❖ The purposes of God are not dependent on any force as much as this force of prayer.

-E. M. Bounds

❖ No one is a firmer believer in the power of prayer than the devil; not that he practices it, but he suffers from it.

-Guy H. King

❖ Woe unto treadmill Christians! Of all people, they need to get into the warm Gulf Stream of prayer.

-Leonard Ravenhill
(RPR, pg. 88)

Likewise, the Spirit also helpeth our infirmities: for we know not what we should pray for as we ought: but the Spirit itself maketh intercession for us with groanings which cannot be uttered. And he that searcheth the hearts knoweth what is the mind of the Spirit, because he maketh intercession for the saints according to the will of God (Romans 8:26-27).

******

The Prayer Journal

I am sure that through the years you have probably been encouraged to keep a prayer journal. In a prayer journal you not only record your requests, but you also make notation of answered prayers.

Like me, it might be hard to keep a prayer journal, because so many prayers are waiting in the recesses of your heart to be addressed by faith at the proper time. Prayerful waiting ensures that your prayers are lifted up by the wings of quiet confidence to be taken to the throne room of God. In a hopeful way, you also quietly wait to see if the same gentle wings eventually catch the wind of God's Spirit and softly land upon your life with His blessed answers.

However, recently Jeannette encouraged me to keep a prayer journal. Sometimes in the midst of great travailing over certain matters, it can be easy to miss the answer to prayers that may not seem as urgent.

That very morning, I had recorded a couple of prayer requests. One such request was that God would put His hand heavily upon the tender heart of a young man who clearly needed to see that his present ways were leading him down a rocky path. I knew that unless God convicted this young man, the meeting I had scheduled with him that very day could prove to be counterproductive.

As I began to contend with this young man, I became aware of his inner struggle. As we talked, I realized that God had indeed put His hand upon this man's tender conscience. In a way he was waiting for someone to help him come to terms with the heaviness so that he could once again have a clean conscience.

It became clear that God had indeed prepared the young man to respond in a beneficial way. At the end of our conversation, he had come to an understanding of the dangerous way in which he was walking, had repented, and was once again at peace with God.

When I came home from meeting with him, I realized that I could record the answer to prayer on the very same day I had prayed about it. Even though the answered prayer did not address some of what I would consider urgent needs on my behalf, it did clearly address what was the main concern of God on that day in regard to this person.

I realize that answered prayers reveal the real concern and heart of God. We must ask ourselves whether or not we just want to see personal matters addressed by God or do we want to be part of addressing the matters of the kingdom of God. I don't know about you, but I prefer to be part of the present matters of God's kingdom. Answered prayers are answered prayers and they confirm your faith in God, as well as confirm His faithfulness to bring about matters that are important in light of eternity at that present time.

And whiles I was speaking, and praying, and confessing my sin and the sin of my people, Israel, and presenting my supplication before the LORD my God, for the holy mountain of my God; Yea, whiles I was speaking in prayer, even the man Gabriel, whom I had seen in the vision at the beginning, being caused to fly swiftly, touched me about the time of the evening oblation (Daniel 9:20-21).

******

Prayers of the Heart

- Lord, add this to all thy blessings. Let me be Born Again. Deny me whatever pleases you, but don't deny me this. Let me be Born from Above. Take away whatever seems good to you. Take my reputation, my fortune, my friends, and my health. But give me the privilege of being Born of the Spirit. Let me be received among the children of God.

-John Wesley

❖ May I always be willing that God should use His own methods with me.

-David Brainerd
(LDD, pg. 108)

❖ Lord, thou knowest all my weakness, my folly, my sin, my utter inefficiency. But here I am. Oh, do thou take me, make me what thou wilt, send me where thou pleasest, do with me what thou seest fit, only let me feel thou are with me, that thou lovest me and employest me, and wilt be glorified by thy work done by thee through me!

-Dr. Robert Reid Kalley

I beseech you therefore, brethren, by the mercies of God, that ye present your bodies a living sacrifice, holy, acceptable unto God, which is your reasonable service (Romans 12:1).

❖ Our daily prayer should be, "Direct my footsteps according to Your Word; let no sin rule over me."

-J. R. Miller

Order my steps in thy word: and let not any iniquity have dominion over me (Psalm 119:133).

❖ O' Prince of Glory, who doest bring Thy sons to glory through the cross. Let us not shrink from suffering, reproach or loss.

-Amy Carmichael

❖ O God, save me from a life of barrenness, following a formal pattern of ethics, and give instead that vital contact of soul with Thy divine life that fruit may be produced, and Life—abundant living—may be known again as the final proof for Christ's message and work.

-James Elliot
(SOA, pg. 55)

Be careful for nothing: but in every thing by prayer and supplication with thanksgiving let your requests be made known unto God (Philippians 4:6).

- ❖ Lord, I don't want to carry burdens others make for me, nor burdens the devil makes for me, nor burdens the church wants to put on me, nor burdens from myself. But I do want to carry the burdens *You* make for me.

  -Molly McPherson
  (RPR, pg 79)

- ❖ Oh, that I had the wings of a dove that I might fly away from sin and corruption and be at rest in God.

  -David Brainerd
  (LDD, pg, 143)

And the peace of God, which passeth all understanding, shall keep your hearts and minds through Christ Jesus (Philippians 4:7).

- ❖ May it please Almighty God to enable me to speak during the time He may allow me this year, to the honour and glory of Jesus Christ, and that I may understand that I am a member of His body—in vital union with the Lord of glory—guided by the Holy Spirit and having always before me what he says;
  - "Without me ye can do nothing;
  - "Ask of me and I will give you all that is needed;
  - "For whosoever shall give a cup of water in my name shall not lose his reward;
  - "I will say unto him, well done good and faithful servant, enter into the joy of thy Lord."

  -Dr. Robert Reid Kalley

- ❖ O Lord, thou givest us everything, at the price of an effort.

  -Leonardo Da Vinci

- ❖ Oh that I could always live to and upon God.

  -David Brainerd
  (LDD, pg, 143)

******

We're Hungry, Lord

We're hungry for something, Lord.
We have so much rich food and cake and candy for ourselves, but we're hungry.
People around us are so stiff and tight and hard to reach.
And they make us that way.
But we're hungry for something more.
People we know keep talking about great ideas, brilliant questions, and the problem of God's existence.
But we're hungry for You, not ideas or theories.
We want You to touch us, to reach inside us and turn us on.
There are so many people who will counsel us to death.
But we're hungry for someone who really knows You and has You, someone who can get so close to us that we can see You there.
We have so many things, but we're hungry for You.
Deep, deep down inside we're hungry, even if we appear to be silly, lazy, or unconcerned at times.
We're hungry for Your kind of power and love and joy.
Feed us, Lord, Feed us with Your rich food.

-Anonymous

❖ I long to be wholly conformed to God and transformed into His image.

-David Brainerd
(LDD, pg. 98)

For whom he did foreknow, he also did predestinate to be conformed to the image of his Son, that he might be the firstborn among many brethren (Romans 8:29).

❖ Oh, that I may feel this continual hunger, and not be retarded, but animated by every cluster from Canaan to reach forward in the narrow way, for the full enjoyment and possession of the heavenly inheritance! Oh, that I may never loiter in my heavenly journey.

-David Brainerd
(LDD, pg. 104)

- Farewell, vain world, my soul. Oh, that God would purge away my dross, and take away my tin, and refine me seven times.

  -David Brainerd

- Keep me. Lord, from fainting in this fierce fight, when the foe is rising, clothe me with Thy might.

  -Evan Roberts

******

Answered Prayer

I asked God for strength,
that I might achieve,
I was made weak,
that I might learn humbly to obey...

I asked for health,
that I might do greater things,
I was given infirmity,
that I might do better things...

I asked for riches,
That I might be happy,
I was given poverty,
That I might be wise...

I asked for power
that I might have the praise of men,
I was given weakness,
That I might feel the need of God...

I asked for all things,
  That I might enjoy life,
I was given life,
  That I might enjoy all things…

I got nothing that I asked for—
But everything I had hoped for;
  Almost despite myself.
  My unspoken prayers were answered.
I am among all men most richly blessed.

-Unknown Confederate Soldier

****

Personal Prayers of the Heart

I have recorded personal prayers of the heart. These heart cries show personal struggle, appreciation, and serious meditation about the matters of life and eternity. It is my hope that such prayers will encourage you.

- Lord, You have provided redemption, yet we shun it to put on some religious cloak and call it salvation. God help us in our delusion. Save us from the consuming fires of our own ignorance, delusion, and rebellion.
- I cannot begin to comprehend O' Lord what you did for me 20 centuries ago so that I could become part of your eternal lineage. How precious You are—never let me forget this fact because in doing so, I will become lost and my life insignificant. You are the only one who makes a person significant in Your kingdom as you did Ruth, Mary, and Joseph. Thank You for Your precious faithfulness.
- Lord, we hide behind your love, sing about it, and talk about it, but in reality we must embrace it by faith if we are going to experience it. Truly, we must stop talking about what we have not experienced and come to the place that we know what Your love feels and tastes like.

- Lord, we make it difficult for ourselves because we love the world too much and love You too little. Without enduring love, we will be unable to make the necessary separation to commit all to You. It is indeed a sad state of affairs.
- Lord, You have given much, but we so often withhold our best from You. You gave Your best, but we only give that which costs us nothing. You call us to Yourself, while we keep our heart aloof from You. You show mercy, and we show ingratitude. You show grace, and we show contempt. Oh Lord, I choose to love and serve You, but save me from my sinful disposition and wicked ways so I can walk in the ways of righteousness and blessings.
- Lord, inaction can be as bad as wrong actions. Inaction is the sin of omission. It tries to remain neutral to maintain popularity. Lord, save me from the logic and justification of inaction when I know what is right and true before You. Give me the courage to do what is right no matter the personal cost.
- Lord, I want to walk in Your ways, but my flesh must be overcome by Your Word, and my prideful glory must give way to Your unfolding glory.
- In my ordinary ways Lord, I want You to show Yourself in extraordinary ways so that You can be glorified in my life.
- Lord, there are so many struggles with the "ifs" and "whys" of life. However, there is one truth that remains constant, and that is You. Help me believe You about forgiveness when the "ifs" of my past life haunt me, and trust You when the "whys" of my present life mock me.
- Lord, I know I must fix my heart on You regardless of my plight. Strengthen my inner man in my weariness, speak to me in depression, revive me in my distress, and enable me to fix my heart on You.
- Lord, it is all about You. As the wise saying goes, "It must be more of You, less of me. However, my heartfelt prayer is that it will be all of You, and none of me."
- Lord, the righteous can call for deliverance, while the needy soul can know redemption. The humble will experience joy and life, while the poor in spirit will encounter salvation. The

sorrowful will know comfort, but the wicked shall be remembered no more. I choose to be on Your side. For you are my strength and hope.

- Lord, You are precious. You are worth the birth pangs, the growing pains, the times of sorrow, the reality of challenges, and the mark of death. In each struggle, we must remember that it will always be about the glorious reality of gaining You.
- Lord, Your greatness is a mystery that is to be discovered by the poor in spirit, the humble in heart, and those who are childlike in faith. Oh Lord, how I desire to possess all of these qualities before You so that I can discover the depth of Your greatness and faithfulness.
- Lord, Christianity is not for the fainthearted. Give me a strong heart towards You and a sound mind to clearly see the way set before me by Your Spirit, Word, and examples.
- Lord, I would rather be considered a fool for believing the Gospel, than proven to be a fool as I perish in unbelief. I would rather embrace the simplicity of the Gospel as a child, rather than be found out to be an intellectual, stiff-necked foe of Yours. I would rather be weak before You so I can discover Your strength, instead of being judged as a reprobate on judgment day. O Lord, the line between a fool and a wise person comes down to believing You. Give me the faith to wisely respond in obedience to your Gospel.
- Lord, we do have the tendency to think too highly of ourselves. We cannot see that our ways are perverted, our conclusions vain, and our activities empty. Lord, I need to regress in my opinion of self in order to progress in the knowledge of You. Do what You have to do to break me in my arrogance.
- Lord, I must humble myself to give way to You in order to stand behind my shield of faith. Therefore, expose and purge me of self-sufficiency so when the time comes, I will not deny even knowing You.
- Lord, how we need to be delivered from sitting on our own throne where the intellect reigns, personal doctrine judges, and fear and speculation become the final authority as to what we consider to be truth. Lord, I want You to reign supremely in my

life so that I will know You as the source of power behind what constitutes truth and life.

- Lord, I have no intention of forgetting why I am here. I am not here to get used to this world, but to become a stranger in it. I can sense my separation from the world because I am becoming restless for home, discontent with where I am, and desirous of being with You in glory.
- Lord, the contrast is obvious. Your wisdom will either prepare my heart so You can make Your ways known to me, or I will give in to the foolishness of my heart. Lord, I want to know You, and not be content to allow my religious ways to establish me on the shifting sands of destruction.
- Lord, each believer's life represents a vineyard. How the vineyard looks and functions will be determined by Your presence and influence in our lives. Lord, I desire You to walk with me in the vineyard of my life.
- Lord, I want to be a watchman in my spiritual life, not a fool in my rebellion. Oh Lord, I know my tendency to rebel, but I also know Your faithfulness. I humble myself before You in repentance for any deviant way, to seek Your intervention in all matters pertaining to life and godliness.
- Lord, I need to seek You early before the voice of self determines my perspective. I need to seek You early before the world demands my devotion and service. I need to seek You early before others influence my perception. Lord, I need to seek You early, because I need You to guide me through the day.
- Lord, the Christian life is a cut above this world. Therefore, I have no reason for living, thinking, and acting like the world. Give me a vision and heart to rise above the world so that I can walk in Your perfect ways.
- Lord, You are all we need. Why do we insist on getting away from the simplicity of our hope in You? I do not want my spiritual life to be wrecked by the waves of disobedience on the rocks of unbelief. Keep me in the current of your Spirit.
- Lord, as believers, we have a humbling past, a blessed present, and a glorious future. We have this complete hope

because of what You did on the cross as our substitute. Thank You for Your unchanging promises that never grow old.

- Lord, I choose to believe You and Your words. I choose to suffer in order to gain, die in order to experience Your life, and overcome the essence of self so that I can obtain a better resurrection in the next life.
- Lord, I know where You found me. I also know You have adorned me in Your redemption with Your righteousness. Therefore, I need to walk in the clothing of humility to ensure I abide in the brightness of Your anointing and glory.
- Lord, we positionally have overcome, we presently have the means to overcome, and one day we will overcome all when we are lifted out of our present life to live forever with You in Your glory. Amen.

Church Matters

- The Church herself, which should be the appeaser of God in all things, what is she but the exasperator of God?

  -Salvian
  (GPQ, pg. 49)

- I am learning the vanity of words. If God does not speak through me, as it is plain He does not through most preachers today, I had better leave off trying to preach.

  -James Elliot
  (SOA, pg. 145)

- In Acts the apostles prayed for 10 days then preached for 10 minutes and 3000 people were saved. Today pastors pray for 10 minutes then preach for 10 days and wonder why no-one is saved.

  -B.H. Clendennen.

And, behold, I send the promise of my Father upon you: but tarry ye in the city of Jerusalem, until ye be endued with power from on high (Luke 24:49).

- Perhaps it would surprise the modern Church to realize that the prejudice of some of its people would still reject John the Baptist's message, their worldly disillusionment would still crucify Jesus Christ, and their self-righteousness would still criticize the Apostle Paul. As we can see, base humanity clothed in self-righteousness has the same capacity today to show ill-will as it did in Jesus' day.

  -RJK

- The tragedy of the modern day Church is that we have misunderstood obedience as legalism.

  -K. P. Yohannan

- Church members in too many cases are like deep sea divers, encased in the suits designed for many fathoms deep, marching bravely to pull out plugs in bath tubs.

  -Peter Marshall
  (JMM, pg. 34)

- The reality is that the true Church of Jesus is made up of those who believe in Jesus Christ. He is the One who serves as the essence of absolute truth. Since truth is eternal, there is no way that mere man or a religious system can conquer its heights, dredge its depths, or travel its width.

  -RJK

- I am convinced that many evangelicals are not truly and soundly converted. Among the evangelicals it is entirely possible to come into membership, to ooze in by osmosis, to leak through the cells of the church and never know what it means to be born of the Spirit and washed in the blood. A great deal that passes for the deeper life is nothing more or less than basic Christianity. There is nothing deeper about it, and it is where we should have been from the start...What we need is what the old Methodists called a sound conversion. There is a difference between conversion and a sound conversion. People who have never been soundly converted do not have the Spirit to enlighten them. When they read the Sermon on the Mount or the teaching passages of the epistles that tell them how to live or the doctrinal passages that tell how they can live, they are unaffected. The Spirit who wrote them is not witnessing in their hearts because they have not been born of the Spirit. That often happens.

  -A W Tozer

And said, Verily I say unto you, Except ye be converted, and become as little children, ye shall not enter into the kingdom of heaven. Whosoever therefore, shall humble himself as this little child, the same is greatest in the kingdom of heaven (Matthew 18:3-4).

- We are playing church. We are so busy trying to be relevant to the world that we have become just like the world..... AND the world is not impressed.

  -Nancy Leigh DeMoss

- The world has lost the power to blush over its vice; the Church has lost her power to weep over it.

  -Leonard Ravenhill
  (RPR, pg. 22)

And while they went to buy, the bridegroom came; and they that were ready went in with him to the marriage: and the door was shut (Matthew 25:10).

- Brethren, the crying sin of the Church is her laziness after God.

  -Samuel Chadwick

- The true man of God is heartsick, grieved at the worldliness of the Church...grieved at the toleration of sin in the Church, grieved at the prayerlessness in the Church. He is disturbed that the corporate prayer of the Church no longer pulls down the strongholds of the devil.

  -Leonard Ravenhill

Ye adulterers and adulteresses, know ye not that the friendship of the world is enmity with God? whosoever therefore will be a friend of the world is the enemy of God (James 4:4).

- Most of the time all we can see are the Demases who run back to the world, while failing to see the Joshuas that have come as far as they dare as a means to personally experience God. We see the Aarons of religion erecting the golden calves of idolatry in the sanctuaries of churches, and not the Noahs who are hidden in the ark of Christ. We see the children of Israel dancing around the altars of idols but do not see the seven thousand who have never bowed their knees to the idols of their present age. Like Jonah who was asleep in the hull of indifference while the storm raged above, we see those who are asleep in the pews of churches as the darkness of the present age slams against the doors of complacency, but we do not see the ones who are hidden in the secret chambers of communion or the obscure caves of God's abiding protection.

-RJK

Yet I have left me seven thousand in Israel, all the knees which have not bowed unto Baal, and every mouth which hath not kissed him (1 Kings 19:18).

❖ The passion for ruling is the mother of heresy.

-John Chrysostom
(GPQ, pg. 129)

❖ The Church is an organism that grows best in an alien society.

-C. Stacey Woods

❖ Dead men need evangelists: living men need pastors and teachers. Apostles, prophets, evangelists are devoted to the *extension* of the church; pastors and teachers to its *edification.* Evangelists are the Christ-given quarrymen who dig out the stones. Pastors are the stone-squarers who take off their rough edges. Teachers are the masons who put the stones in place.

-Herbert Lockyer
(MP, pg. 180)

❖ The invasion of the Church by the world is a menace to the extension of Christ's Kingdom. In all ages conformity to the world by Christians has resulted in lack of spiritual life and a consequent lack of spiritual vision and enterprise. A secularized or self-centered Church can never evangelize the world.

-John R. Mott

Where there is no vision, the people perish: but he that keepth the law, happy is he (Proverbs 29:18).

- ❖ The neglected heart will soon be a heart overrun with worldly thoughts; the neglected life will soon become a moral chaos; the church that is not jealously protected by mighty intercession and sacrificial labors will before long become the abode of every evil bird and the hiding place for unsuspected corruption. The creeping wilderness will soon take over that church that trusts in its own strength and forgets to watch and pray.

-A. W. Tozer

Watch ye therefore, and pray always, that ye may be accounted worthy to escape all these things that shall come to pass, and to stand before the Son of man (Luke 21:36).

- ❖ The church today needs praying people to meet the fearful crisis that is facing her.

-E. M. Bounds

- ❖ Today's church wants to be raptured from responsibility.

-Leonard Ravenhill

- ❖ The Church has in her keeping the secrets of prayer and meditation and communion with the risen Christ, but perhaps she has kept them in the icebox of orthodoxy.

-Peter Marshall
(JMM, pg.160)

- ❖ Men are God's method. The Church is looking for better methods; God is looking for better men.

-E.M. Bounds

- ❖ One hundred religious persons knit into a unity by careful organization do not constitute a church any more than eleven dead men make a football team. The first requisite is life, always.

-A. W. Tozer

The thief cometh not, but to steal, and to kill, and to destroy: I am come that they might have life, and that they might have it more abundantly (John 10:10).

- Jesus didn't save us to sit, slumber, or continue in sin. He saved us to serve, and that means we will be called to confront and overcome the works of darkness whenever and wherever it is encountered. We may want to go AWOL, but we are to be the salt and the light of the world until His return. God's Church needs to shake herself awake and take hold of the true power that causes demons to tremble.

  -Jeannette Haley

- As part of this Body, I have come to recognize that all of our pursuits for truth according to higher learning and denominational influences have made us expert debaters of the Word rather than lovers of it. We are not richer for our theological understandings and differences. We are poorer for them. In fact, we are missing the simplicity behind the order and function of the Body of Christ.

  -RJK

- The standard of practical holy living has been so low among Christians that the least degree of real devotedness of life and walk is looked upon with surprise and often even with disapprobation by a large portion of the Church. And, for the most part, the followers of the Lord Jesus Christ are satisfied with a life so conformed to the world, and so like it in almost every respect, that, to a causal observer, no difference is discernible.

  -Hannah Whitall Smith
  (CHL, pg. 205)

And be not conformed to this world: but be ye transformed by the renewing of your mind, that ye may prove what is that good, and acceptable, and perfect, will of God (Romans 12:2).

- A. W. Tozer wrote that the failure in current evangelism lies in its humanistic approach. He described much of the activity among Christians as "motion without progress".

- Today there is so much physical comfort for the pray-ers. (Our churches are more air-conditioned than prayer-conditioned, and are well-heated too.)

  -Leonard Ravenhill

- Are not the Church in their present state a standing, public, perpetual denial of the gospel? Do they not stand out before the world, as a living, unanswerable contradiction of the gospel; and do more to harden sinners and lead them into a spirit of caviling and infidelity, than all the efforts of professed infidels from the beginning of the world to the present day? A revival of real praying would produce a spiritual revolution.

  -E.M. Bounds

- In considering the Church, I can see how some of its members operate in extremes. If they are not ignorant about the things of God, they are ridiculous. If they are not complacent, they are fanatics. If they are not asleep, they are unrealistic. The major problem in the Church is that people have not been properly trained or discipled.

  -RJK

- It is a poor sermon that gives no offense; that neither makes the hearer displeased with himself nor with the preacher."

  -George Whitefield

- Some preachers ought to put more fire into their sermons or more sermons into the fire.

  -Vance Havner

❖ I am growing more and more aware that all too often we preachers aim at nothing and hit it.

-Peter Marshall
(JMM, pg. 20)

❖ We try organizing - we should try agonizing.

-Leonard Ravenhill

❖ How sadly and how slowly I am learning that loud preaching and long preaching are not substitutes for inspired preaching.

-James Elliot
(SOA, pg. 156)

❖ Many groups attempt to break out of the mold set by denominations and institutions and seek to try new things, yet end up making the same mistake. They are not based on heavenly realities as found in Christ. They are not radical enough in their pursuit of original Christian reality.

-Manfred Haller

❖ The Church of Christ has been founded by shedding its own blood not that of others...

-Jerome
(GPQ, pg. 50)

❖ The church upon its knees would bring heaven upon earth.

-E. M. Bounds
(WOP, pg. 66)

❖ "I have nothing and possess all things."... The church today has everything yet possesses nothing.

-Leonard Ravenhill

Because thou sayest, I am rich, and increased with goods, and have need of nothing; and knowest not that thou art wretched, and miserable, and poor, and blind, and naked (Revelation 3:17).

******

A Challenge

The visible Church appears as if it is becoming powerless and lost in the midst of man's various inspired doctrines, movements, and entertainment. Sadly, much of the Church stands naked, stripped of its armor, and unable to withstand the attacks of the devil and the onslaught of the powers and rulers of darkness.

Without power and authority, many will not be able to stand in the midst of wickedness. Although there are those in the organized Church that claim they have the armor in place, it is clearly missing. The belt of truth has become tarnished with compromise and the breastplate of righteousness weak with worldliness. The feet are becoming lame and tormented because the power of the Gospel is absent, while the shield of faith has been rendered into a pretty paper shield of pseudo-faiths that blow away with every wind of doctrine.

The helmet of salvation is no longer in place. It has been put aside to accept the false security of man's coverings or the latest attempts to make himself righteous, holy, or immortal. The sword has been rendered useless, dissected in many pieces in the name of intellectual and religious pursuits for so-called "truth" and sadly replaced with man's watered-down Bible versions, traditions, and theology.

******

❖ Oh, the need there is for present-day preachers to have their lips touched with a live coal from the altar of God!

-E. M. Bounds

Then flew one of the seraphims unto me, having a live coal in his hand, which he had taken with the tongs from off the altar: And he laid it upon my mouth, and said, Lo, this hath touched thy lips, and thine iniquity is taken away, and they sin purged (Isaiah 6:6-7).

- Finney preached, and sometimes the whole congregation would get up and leave! That's good preaching.

  -Leonard Ravenhill

- The Church has only this task: to embody Christ, manifest His nature, demonstrate God's love to the world, and proclaim His Lordship over all things.

  -Manfred Haller
  (CA, pg. 156)

- The Church in America is creating a McDonald's type of atmosphere with its abundance, while the true ministers of the Gospel are often being sacrificed on the altars of persecution and poverty. No doubt the rewards of these godly ministers of the Gospel will be great, but how does God look at a Church that gives Him the crumbs of indifference, while it feasts at the table of abundance and worldliness?

  -RJK

- (This statement was made in relationship to doctoring the Gospel) A little truth is given up, and then a little more, and men fill up the vacuum with opinions, inferences, speculations, and dreams, till their wine is mixed with water, and the water none of the best. Many preachers, and I speak it with sorrow have built a tower of theological speculations, upon which they sit like Nero, fiddling the tune of their own philosophy while the world is burning with sin and misery. They are playing with the toys of speculation while men's souls are being lost.

  -Charles Spurgeon

Beware lest any man spoil you through philosophy and vain deceit, after the tradition of men, after the rudiments of the world, and not after Christ (Colossians 2:8).

- There is a lot of soft, sentimental talk about Him today that brings no conviction. When Isaiah saw the Lord, he did not feel comfortable! Neither did Habakkuk nor Daniel nor Paul nor John. We want a picture of Him today that does not disturb us, that smiles at sin, and winks at iniquity. I remember a man who told me he wanted to hear no hell-fire sermons but rather about the meek and lowly Jesus. Yet the poor man did not seem to realize that the meek and lowly Jesus said more about hell than is reported from the lips of anyone else in the Bible! We need a true and complete vision of God in His holiness and Christ in His glory that will bring us to repentance."

-Vance Havner

❖ The modern Church has gone to extremes in its effort to overcompensate for decades of hellfire and brimstone, legalistic preaching. What has been lost in the process is the Bible's definition of sin, and what constitutes true repentance, godly living, and salvation. What is left for most people today is a 'Kool Whip' belief system that encourages a lazy type of comfortable religious experience. This sugary diet has left people spiritually emaciated. Even milk is hard for them to swallow. Most preaching that one encounters today is nothing but regurgitated MUSH!

-Jeannette Haley

I tell you, Nay; but, except ye repent, ye shall all likewise perish (Luke 13:3).

❖ The Church must come back to center because it has lost its way. It is no better for its endless education or theological debates. It is not more powerful because of its divisions or more respected because of its incessant demand of being right about certain spiritual matters. The Church needs to cease being a parasite that feeds on the pride or ignorance of others to prove a senseless spiritual point. Rather, it needs to regain the heavenly vision of how each member is meant to function for the benefit of the whole Body for the glory of God.

-RJK

But speaking the truth in love, may grow up into him in all things, which is the head, even Christ: From whom the whole body fitly joined together and compacted by that which every joint supplieth, according to the effectual working in the measure of every part, maketh increase of the body unto the edifying of itself in love (Ephesians 4:15-16).

A Matter of His Power and Glory

❖ We must follow the same path of judgments as Jesus did to realize the glory of God. In the Garden of Gethsemane, our humanity will only be poured out as we exchange our will for the will of God. At Gabbatha, our flesh must lose in order for God's perfect plan to have its way. At Golgatha, the total essence of our life (rights and identity) must be offered up in order to possess the life of Jesus.

-RJK

❖ Happiness is a subordinate consideration which He assigns to the final and essential end of His glory.

-Fenelon
(TWG, pg. 33)

❖ All of creation tells of God's power and majesty, but without His presence, it truly is hell.

-Jeannette Haley

❖ I found the comfort of being a Christian and counted the sufferings of the present life not worthy to be compared with the glory of divine enjoyments even in this world.

-David Brainerd
(LDD, pg. 127)

❖ The glory of Christ *in* us will change our perception, our ways, and our countenance. The glory of Christ *through* us will reveal the liberty of the Spirit in our lives. It is the glory of Jesus that *reflects outwardly* from our lives that will verify the truths in our lives of all that is written. Such glory will declare that all such matters are indeed true, glorious, and eternal.

-RJK

And if children, then heirs; heirs of God, and joint heirs with Christ; if so be that we suffer with him, that we may be also glorified together (Romans 8:17).

- God's glory is His holiness. To glorify God is to yield oneself so that God may show forth His glory in us.

  -Andrew Murray

- The gospel has nothing to do with entertaining the flesh or relieving the sinner of circumstances that his sin has induced. It has everything to do with declaring the holiness of God, the depravity of the human condition, and of the awful price that Jesus paid to reconcile fallen sinners to an impeccable God. It is a message to sober the frivolous, to humble the proud, to awaken the indifferent and careless ones; a message to break the blasphemer, silence the scoffer, and to cause the sinner to repent. It is a message to prepare new creatures for heaven, not rehabilitate sinners to live more comfortably on the earth or more prosperously in this world.

  -Dick York
  Missionary and founder of
  Shield of Faith Mission International.

Therefore if any man be in Christ, he is a new creature: old things are passed away; behold, all things are become new (2 Corinthians 5:17).

- God's strength is used for one means: to carry out His eternal plan in regard to His creation and man's salvation. We see His strength restrained in mercy, channeled in grace, disciplined in sanctification, powerful in miracles, and mighty in wrath.

  -RJK

- Eternity to the godly is a day that has no sunset; eternity to the wicked is a night that has no sunrise.

  -Thomas Watson

- Oh, the closest walk with God is the sweetest heaven that can be enjoyed on earth!

  -David Brainerd
  (LDD, pg. 86)

******

I am blessed!
Can you feel it?
Its there—the breeze,
the wing span—the cool air,
the sun shining on air.
Lightness, hope, everlasting,
the joy of freedom at last.
My soul doth sing with harmony
the song of life, the spirit of hope.
My heart calls out to you O Lord!
Guide me on your everlasting arms
and carry me.
I am blessed!

-Maureen Human

- Before the Lord will move in power, our orthodoxy will have to be stabbed, our conventions shattered, and our stony hearts again know tears. Only a small portion of the Church will conceive in the Holy Ghost; but later, the whole body of the Church will feel the birth.

  -Leonard Ravenhill

- We all want to have mountaintop experiences with God, but we want to avoid the preparation that first must take place in the barren wildernesses of our lives. The reality is that as Christians, we are not meant to live in and for mountaintop experiences. Rather, we are meant to walk through the valleys of humiliation so that we can share and become identified in our Lord's glory. It is one thing to experience His glory, and another to share in His glory.

-RJK

And he said, I beseech thee, shew me thy glory (Exodus 33:18).

- The world is a dark, cloudy mansion. Oh, when will the Sun of Righteousness shine on my soul without intermission?

  -David Brainerd
  (LDD, pg. 138)

- To the self-denying spirit, the will and glory of God and the salvation of man are always to be more important than our own interests or pleasure.

  -Andrew Murray

- In the first chapter of the first book of Timothy, Paul summarizes his adoration for Jesus by declaring, "Now unto the King eternal, immortal, invisible, the only wise God, be honour and glory for ever and ever. Amen" (1:17). What a glorious picture of Jesus! The fact that people would exchange this revelation with fables and heresies, replace a pure heart with a religious façade, charity with dead rituals, and faith with traditions, is a tragedy that amounts to a spiritual shipwreck.

  -RJK

******

The Legend of the Cornerstone

The Bible refers to Jesus as the cornerstone who was rejected by the builders. It is important to point out that all stones in a building are shaped according to the cornerstone. The Word of God clearly brings out that Jesus is the only cornerstone to true religion.

According to Ironside's commentary on Acts, the Scriptures in regard to the rejection of the cornerstone were in reference to a legend. When the temple of Solomon was under construction, the builders discovered an odd shaped stone. Since they felt it had not been shaped like the other stones, they concluded it was a mistake and rolled it down into the valley of Kidron, which was located below the temple area.

Seven years later the builders needed the cornerstone to complete the temple. To their surprise they discovered that the odd shaped stone they had discarded was the actual cornerstone. They had to ascend into Kidron valley and locate the stone that they had rejected. When they located it, the stone was covered by lichens and debris. They had to resurrect it to complete the temple.

Like the cornerstone of the temple, Jesus did not fit into the religious scene. The religious leaders of the day rejected Him. They marred Him with their anger and hate, and cast Him into the grave. However, three days later He rose from the grave with a new, glorified body. Like the cornerstone of old, without Jesus a person's life will never be completed. Such a life will never make sense or ultimately display the beauty of God's design.

******

Wherefore also it is contained in the scripture, Behold, I lay in Sion a chief corner stone, elect, precious: and he that believeth on him shall not be confounded. Unto you therefore which believe he is precious: but unto them which be disobedient, the stone which the builders disallowed, the same is made the head of the corner. (1 Peter 2:6-7).

- Oh, to be truly a man of God! A man who knows and proves these three things: God is all; God claims all; God works all.

  -Andrew Murray

- We want to be clothed upon with power; God wants to strip us. We want power; He wants to expose our weakness. We want large bonuses for small investments of prayer. We want to sow radish seeds but reap a forest of redwoods.

-Leonard Ravenhill

- In the will of God we have the highest expression of His divine perfection, and at the same time the high energy of His divine power.

-Andrew Murray

- In Ezekiel 1, the prophet saw God in living color. His brightness had to be immense. His likeness was simple, but represented His authority (lion), His strength (ox), His representation or glory (man), and His heavenly perspective (eagle). His leadership clearly proves to be universal and unlimited. He moves only in compliance with the Spirit. There is agreement in the Spirit as to what He must do, how He must do it, and where it will be fulfilled. As God, He will not take detours from His plan.

-RJK

Their wings were joined one to another; they turned not when they went; they went every one straight forward. As for the likeness of their faces, they four had the face of a man, and the face of a lion, on the right side: and they four had the face of an ox on the left side; they four also had the face of an eagle (Ezekiel 1:9-10).

The Declaration of Creation

- The visible order of the universe proclaims a supreme intelligence.

-Jean-Jacques Rousseau

- Of what I call God, And fools call Nature.

-Robert Browning

The fool hath said in his heart, There is no God. Corrupt are they, and have done abominable iniquity: there is none that doeth good (Psalm 53:1).

❖ It is vital to realize that the first man, Adam, made creation complete. However, due to redemption the second man, Christ, makes man complete.

-RJK

❖ I am in the habit of *walking* on the earth, not *worshipping* it.

-Clement of Alexandria
(DCB, pg, 547)

And changed the glory of the incorruptible God into an image made like to corruptible man, and birds, and four-footed beasts, and creeping things (Romans 1:23).

❖ The creation of man was to be God's masterpiece.

-Andrew Murray

****

And We Had Fun

One would wonder in what way God would enjoy the creation of man when He had heaven with all of its beauty, as well as the adoration of angels to take pleasure in. It's simple. God would enjoy the handiwork of His creation of the earth by enjoying man. He would enjoy man as he personally related and responded to the perfect atmosphere the Lord had placed him within. God would rejoice as man communed with Him. He would find the greatest type of pleasure as man served as His unhindered mirror in the midst of His creation.

My co-laborer in the Gospel, Jeannette Haley, confirmed this pleasure created by the existence of man in the Garden of Eden. Jeannette is a professional artist. Her love for the beauty and detail of creation inspired much of her art. One day she was looking at the beauty of a duck on a postage stamp and noticed the Latin name for it. She began to think about the many different species of ducks. This brought her back to the man who named all of the different species of animals in the beginning: Adam. She was thinking how intelligent he had to have been to name the vast array of different types of animal life. As she pondered how God brought each animal to Adam to be named, the Lord sovereignly broke through her thoughts by saying, "And, we had fun."

And out of the ground the LORD God formed every beast of the field, and every fowl of the air; and brought them unto Adam to see what he would call them: And whatsoever Adam called every living creature, that was the name thereof (Genesis 2:19).

- I can see how it might be possible for a man to look down upon earth and be an atheist, but I cannot conceive how he could look up into the heavens and say there is no God.

  -Abraham Lincoln

- As a house implies a builder; and a garment a weaver, and a door a carpenter, so does the existence of the Universe imply a Creator.

  -Marquis de Vauvenargues

For the invisible things of him from the creation of the world are clearly seen, being understood by the things that are made, even his eternal power and Godhead; so that they are without excuse: Because that, when they knew God, they glorified him not as God, neither were thankful; but became vain in their imaginations, and their foolish heart was darkened (Romans 1:20-21).

- It is impossible to account for the creation of the universe without the agency of a Supreme Being.

  -George Washington

- This cry for "wings" is as old as humanity. Our souls were made to "mount up with wings." And, they can never be satisfied with anything short of flying.

  -Hannah Whitall Smith

But they that wait upon the LORD shall renew their strength; they shall mount up with wings as eagles; they shall run, and not be weary; and they shall walk, and not faint (Isaiah 40:31).

******

A forest I saw
Light glimmering through
Gentle breezes blow
Leaves dancing carelessly

Deep breaths I take
Exhilaration!
Hands reach out to touch
the sky
I feel

I am a part of creation
Twirl and twirl
Freedom
I am loved.

-Maureen Human

- The visible marks of extraordinary wisdom and power appear so plainly in all the works of the creation that a rational creature, who will but seriously reflect on them, cannot miss the discovery of a Deity.

-John Locke

- So irresistible are these evidences of an intelligent and powerful Agent that, of the infinite numbers of men who have exited thro' all the time, they have believed, in the proportion of a million at least to Unit in the hypothesis of an eternal pre-existence of a creator, rather than in that of a self-existent Universe.

-Thomas Jefferson

In the beginning God created the heaven and the earth (Genesis 1:1).

- The more I study nature, the more I stand amazed at the work of the Creator.

-Louis Pasteur

❖ Nature is the art of God.

-Dante Alighieri

******

See the nightingale
As she goes-gliding
Over the mystical waters
From whence cometh her song!
The night light from above
Giving a shimmering ray of reflection of peace.
Hope is her.
My heart signs a new song.
My spirit has finally come alive!
I feel—I feel.

-Maureen Human

Worship

❖ Prayer is preoccupation with our needs. Praise is preoccupation with our blessings. Worship is preoccupation with God himself."

- Leonard Ravenhill

❖ As His people, we must seek the Lord early to worship Him. We indeed need to start our day with His perspective to ensure righteousness in our ways, life in our pursuits, hope in our future, and salvation in our present.

-RJK

With my soul have I desired thee in the night; yea, with my spirit within me will I seek thee early; for when thy judgments are in the earth, the inhabitants of the world will learn righteousness (Isaiah 26:9).

❖ What is the difference between the moral law and the Gospel? The law requires that we worship God as our Creator; the Gospel, that we worship Him in and through Christ. God in Christ is propitious;

out of Him we may see God's power, justice, and holiness: in Him we see His mercy displayed.

-Thomas Watson
(PDC, pg. 319)

❖ A man can no more diminish God's glory by refusing to worship Him than a lunatic can put out the sun by scribbling the word, "darkness" on the walls of his cell.

-C.S. Lewis

❖ Worship renews the spirit as sleep renews the body.

-Richard Clarke Cabot

❖ This is true worship: when the mind of a worshipper presents itself as an undefiled offering to God.

-Lactantius
(DCB, pg, 550)

But the hour cometh, and now is, when the true worshippers shall worship the Father in spirit and in truth: for the Father seeketh such to worship him (John 4:23).

❖ How do we react towards a God of such majesty? Daniel 6:26-27 tells us we must fear Him. In essence, we must dread meeting Him at any point other than repentance, redemption, and righteousness. Repentance is expressed in humility, redemption in submission, and righteousness in obedient faith.

-RJK

❖ Worship is the highest and noblest act that any person can do. When men worship, God is satisfied! "The Father seeketh such to worship Him." Amazing, isn't it? And when you worship, you are fulfilled! Think about this: why did Jesus Christ come? He came to make worshippers out of rebels. We who were once self-centered have to be completely changed so that we can shift our attention outside of ourselves and become able to worship Him.

-Raymond C. Ortlund
(HFG, pg. 333)

❖ The problem with much of the worship today is that it is fleshy. Anytime worship is fleshly, it points to the flesh getting caught up with its sensational and sentimental ways. In other words, instead of worshipping in the right spirit in light of truth, people are getting caught up with how worship is making them feel. Worship is not about feelings, but honoring God. It is about coming into a place of sweet communion and enjoying the reality of who He is. Such revelation does not come from fleshly zeal or sentiment, but from the premise of humility and sobriety.

-RJK

O come, let us worship and bow down; let us kneel before the LORD our maker. For he is our God; and we are the people of his pasture, and the sheep of his hand. Today if ye will hear his voice (Psalm 95:6-7).

The Conflict

- There cannot be a victory unless first there comes a battle.

  -Cyprian
  (DCB, 549)

- Sin will reign if it can: it cannot be satisfied with any place below the throne of the heart.

  -Charles Spurgeon

- It seems to me that behind every sin, every vice, every mess, is a lack of self-discipline...of God's discipline.

  -Peter Marshall
  (JMM, pg. 133)

- The desire for spiritual power and supernatural experiences is the common denominator between Christians and non-Christians alike.

  -Jeannette Haley

- The old man in us will confess and process sin on an intellectual basis and call it repentance. He will outwardly comply with religious codes and call it righteousness. He will play dead and call it humility. He will act rehabilitated and call it godliness. Regardless of the religious cloaks he may wear, the unregenerate disposition of the old man will remain unchanged as long as pride remains unbroken by the powerful conviction of the Spirit of God.

  -RJK

- Do not put it (sin) behind you, or God will put it in front of you.

  -Augustine
  (GPQ, pg. 59)

- The generality of men make light of sin; and he that has slight thoughts of sin, had never great thoughts of God. Indeed, men's undervaluing of sin arises their contempt of God.

  -John Owens

Whosoever is born of God doth not commit sin; for his seed remaineth in him: and he cannot sin, because he is born of God (1 John 3:9).

- How can you pull down strongholds of Satan if you don't even have the strength to turn off your TV?

  -Leonard Ravenhill

- We are commanded to be lords over not only the wild beasts outside of us, but also over the wild lusts within ourselves.

  -Clement of Alexandria
  (DCB, pg. 548)

- We all start out like Cain. We desire to rule ourselves. Granted, Cain may have built the first city, pointing to man's government and civilization, but he had to leave the presence of God to do so.

  -RJK

- It's a natural tendency of our fallen human condition to be religious. Before the fall, Adam and Eve had fellowship with their Creator. After the fall, however, this relationship was lost and fallen man substituted religion for relationship. Adam and Eve sewed fig leaves together to form a covering for their nakedness. Ever since that time, down through the centuries, people have naturally depended upon their own "coverings" and works of righteousness.

  -Jeannette Haley

- Undoubtedly, we have improved means—but unfortunately, we have not improved ends. We have better ways of getting there, but we have no better places to go. We can save more time, but we are not making any better use of the time we save. Everyone agrees that we have made far more advances in the scientific world than we have made in the world of morals and ethics.

-Peter Marshall
(JMM, pg. 64)

- Worrying is carrying tomorrow's load with today's strength--carrying two days at once. It is moving into tomorrow ahead of time. Worrying doesn't empty tomorrow of its sorrow, it empties today of its strength.

-Corrie Ten Boom

Therefore, I say unto you, Take no thought for your life, what ye shall eat, or what ye shall drink; nor yet for your body, what ye shall put on. Is not the life more than meat, and the body than raiment (Matthew 6:25)?

- The problem for many of us in the Christian world is that we have become religious instead of children of God. We have become fleshly and politically correct, rather than spiritual. We have become judgmental, rather than compassionate. We have become gods of our worlds, rather than servants of the Most High God.

-RJK

- If they had a social gospel in the days of the prodigal son, somebody would have given him a bed and a sandwich and he never would have gone home.

-Vance Havner

And when he came to himself, he said, How many hired servants of my father's have bread enough and to spare, and I perish with hunger! I will arise and go to my father, and will say unto him, Father, I have sinned against heaven, and before thee (Luke 15:17-18).

- We manufacture atheists with mundane Christianity.

-Robert Wurtz II

❖ There is no partiality in God's eyes, for He has made everything and everyone. The rich do not impress Him nor does he overlook the poor. God has made everything to be in balance. The rich are to be good stewards of what God has given, while the poor are to be good servants with what they receive. Sadly, balance is lacking in this world, and, where balance is missing, you will find the foolish, the simple, the scorner, the slothful, and those who are angry and contentious about the reality of their vain, unproductive lives.

-RJK

Let your moderation be known unto all men. The Lord is at hand (Philippians 4:5).

❖ First we practice sin, then defend it, then boast of it.

-Thomas Manton

❖ We know that sin and its cohorts of the flesh, self, and the world enslave people into their different delusions. However, sin never promised liberty. It only promises that you can experience all the world can offer without any restraints, while being utterly incapable of sparing you of the consequences. The world promises temporary happiness, but not satisfaction. The flesh promises temporary satisfaction, but never lasting contentment. Self promises temporary exaltation, but never any real peace.

-RJK

❖ God takes away the world, that the heart may cleave more to Him in sincerity.

-Thomas Watson

❖ Repentance always implies hatred of sin. It is feeling towards sin exactly as God feels. It always implies forsaking sin.

-Charles Finney

❖ To learn how to hear the voice of Jesus, He must lead us away from the dictates of pride, the influence of the flesh, and the seductive ways of the world. He will lead us from the self-serving life we are used to so we can learn what it means to walk under His light yoke of love and the easy burden of loving obedience. We must truly get in step with our Lord. But, in order to do this, we must exchange the unrealistic yoke of the self-life and the heavy burden of this present world with Jesus' yoke. His yoke will bring discipline to our walk and His burden will discipline our focus.

-RJK

❖ The world is Satan's bait. He seldom throws out a naked hook... But he conceals the hook in a godly bait, and like a skillful angler, he knows how to use the temptation best suited to our palate.

-Arthur Jackson

❖ Temptation is the proposition presented to the mind that you can satisfy a good appetite in a forbidden way. Temptation *leads* to sin.

-Paris Reidhead
(FRG, pg. 141)

But every man is tempted, when he is drawn away of his own lust, and enticed. Then when lust hath conceived, it bringeth forth sin: and sin, when it is finished, bringeth forth death (James 1:14-15).

❖ (The devil) hath an apple for Eve, a grape for Noah, a change of raiment for Gehazi, a bag for Judas. He can dish out his meat for all palates.

-William Jenkyn
(PDC, pg. 201)

❖ Self is the power of Satan living and working in us, the sad continuation of that first turning from God that was the whole reason for the fall of our first father.

-William Law
(WRP, pg, 34)

❖ Just look at us. Everything is backwards; everything is upside down. Doctors destroy health, lawyers destroy justice, universities destroy knowledge, governments destroy freedom, the major media destroy information and religions destroy spirituality.

- Michael Ellner

- A sin of infirmity may admit apology; a sin of ignorance may find an excuse; but a sin of defiance can find no defense.

  -Sir Richard Baker
  (PDC, pg. 240)

- Inaction is the sin of omission. It tries to remain neutral to maintain popularity with the world instead of doing what is right in order to please God.

  -RJK

Therefore to him that knoweth to do good, and doeth it not, to him it is sin (James 4:17).

- We have to remember that first of all, Satan is the enemy of God .... he's our enemy only because of "collateral damage." Anywhere the Spirit of God is in operation, he feels intimidated and challenged ...... and rightfully so!!!

  - Anna Schwery

- Sin proceeds only when deception goes before it.

  -John Owens
  (ST, pg. 36)

- Sometimes the sins we commit are not moral ones but spiritual. We cultivate a legal attitude toward God, and that's wrong. Christians start out in the Spirit, but when it comes to daily living, we try to perfect ourselves by the flesh.

  -Joni Erickson Tada

Wherefore the law was our schoolmaster to bring us unto Christ, that we might be justified by faith. But after that faith is come, we are no longer under a schoolmaster (Galatians 3:24-25).

❖ Self-justification—the tendency to call a wrong thing right is always strong. It is an ancient bent in human nature.

-Paris Redihead
(FRG, pg. 77)

❖ My enemy is not the unknown future in this world, but Satan who seeks to destroy my faith in God through fear. For God already inhabits the unknown for He is the Alpha and the Omega. Therefore, what I fear I need not fear for He is there.

-Jeannette Haley

❖ (You) were not ashamed to sin but now are ashamed to confess.

-Pacian of Barcelona
(GPQ, pg. 58)

If we confess our sins, he is faithful and just to forgive us our sins, and to cleanse us from all unrighteousness (1 John 1:9).

❖ The religious camps of today are producing militants who are drunk with causes, but who do not know the real voice of Jesus Christ. They are producing religious zealots who cannot discern the truth because they do not love the truth. They are encouraging spiritualism, rather than obedience to the Word of God. They are replacing transformation with outward conformity to religious codes and agendas.

-RJK

******

Reluctance to Repent

I feel when I have sinned an immediate reluctance to go to Christ. I am ashamed to go. I feel as if it would not do to go, as if it were making Christ the minister of sin, to go straight from the swine-trough to the best robe, and a thousand other excuses. But I am persuaded they are all lies direct from hell. John argues the opposite way-'If any man sins, we have an advocate with the Father;' ... The holy sensitiveness of the soul that shrinks from the touch of sin, the acute susceptibility of the conscience at the slightest shade of guilt, will of necessity draw the spiritual mind frequently to the blood of Jesus. And herein lies the secret of a heavenly walk. Acquaint yourself with it, my reader, as the most precious secret of your life. He who lives in the habit of a prompt and minute acknowledgement of sin, with his eye reposing calmly, believingly, upon the crucified Redeemer, soars in spirit where the eagle's pinion [wings] range not.

-Octavius Winslow

Having therefore brethren, boldness to enter into the holiest by the blood of Jesus, By a new living way, which he hath consecrated for us, through the veil, that is to say, his flesh; And having an high priest over the house of God; Let us draw near with a true heart in full assurance of faith, having our hearts sprinkled from an evil conscience, and our bodies washed with pure water (Hebrews 10:19-22).

- Many pastors criticize me for taking the Gospel so seriously. But do they really think that on Judgment Day, Christ will chastise me, saying, 'Leonard, you took Me too seriously?

-Leonard Ravenhill

- So desperately wicked and so deceitful are the hearts of men that they flatter themselves by living in their sins until they come to their last breath. Thousands really believe they have found a way to live. But it is a broad way and will lead them to destruction.

-John Wesley

Enter ye in at the strait gate: for wide is the gate, and broad is the way, that leadeth to destruction, and many there be which go in thereat (Matthew 7:13).

- All it takes to make a preacher is a sermon - but it takes an altar to make a man of God.

-B.H. Clendennen

We have an altar, whereof they have no right to eat which serve the tabernacle. For the bodies of those beasts, whose blood is brought into the sanctuary by the high priest for sin, are burned without the camp (Hebrews 13:10-11).

- A man who spoke little English gave this description of a sermon he had heard: he said 'Big wind. Much lightning. Loud thunder. No rain!

  -Selected

- The devil doesn't mind how many sermons we preach or prepare if it will keep us from preparing ourselves.

  -Vance Havner.

- No one can be a good preacher to the people who is not willing to preach in a manner that seems childish and vulgar to some.

  -Martin Luther

- If Jesus had preached the same message that ministers preach today, He would never have been crucified.

  -Leonard Ravenhill

As it is written, Behold, I lay in Sion a stumblingstone and rock of offence; and whosoever believeth on him shall not be ashamed (Romans 9:33).

- The great number of teachers is the reason of the multitude of sects, for which we shall soon have no names left.

  -Jan Amos Comenius

- A popular evangelist reaches your emotions. A true prophet reaches your conscience.

  -Leonard Ravenhill

- It is not our business to make the message acceptable, but to make it available. We are not to see that they like it, but that they get it.

  -Dr. Vance Havner

- Legal Christians do not deny Christ; they only seek to add something to Christ. Their idea is, Christ and—something besides.

  -Hannah Whitall Smith

- So, then, we are called atheists. We confess that we are atheists as far as false gods are concerned but not with respect to the true God.

  -Justin
  (GPQ, pg. 47)

- The vanity of the world brings its own bondage. It promises, but all it can do is torment. It offers purpose, only to prove to be fleeting. Such vanity shows itself in a false glory that quickly gives way to emptiness. The world has no lasting form; therefore, there is no real order to be found in its ways or results.

  -RJK

- Whenever my mind is taken off of the things of this world and set on God, my soul is then at rest.

  -David Brainerd
  (LDD, pg. 131)

Thou wilt keep him in perfect peace, whose mind is stayed on thee: because he trusteth in thee (Isaiah 26:3).

- But he who lives in the visible wants his honor to be vindicated at once here below. He who lives in the eternal is satisfied to leave the vindication of his rights and honor in God's hands.

  -Andrew Murray

- The abandonment of evil things, then, consists in refusing them with horror. The abandonment of good things consists in using them for our needs in moderation, continually seeking to refuse those imaginary needs with which greedy nature would flatter itself.

  -Fenelon
  (TWG, pg. 43)

- Fearful is our danger, but joyful is our security. The man whom God upholds, devils cannot throw down.

-Charles Spurgeon
(FCB, pg. 47)

- Be pleasing to Him whose soldiers you are, and whose pay you receive. May none of you be found to be a deserter. Let your baptism be your armament; your faith, your helmet; your love, your spear; your endurance, your full suit of armour.

-Ignatius
(GPQ, pg. 47)

Put on the whole armour of God, that ye may be able to stand against the wiles of the devil (Ephesians 6:11).

- Nothing lies heavier upon me than the misimprovement of time.

-David Brainerd
(LDD, pg. 143)

- The most specious and glorious pretence made to an acquaintance with the Father without holiness and obedience to His commandments, serves only to prove the pretenders to be liars. The love of the world and of the Father dwell not together.

-John Owens

Love not the world, neither the things that are in the world. If any man love the world, the love of the Father is not in him (1 John 2:15).

- When people are down, others will exalt and honor themselves above these wrestling souls. They will take the absence of such challenges in their own lives as a signal of their so-called "goodness" or "elitism". Such logic is foolish, but man's speculations prove to be nothing more than folly.

-RJK

- A truly unworldly, heavenly spirit manifests itself not so much in the desire to leave earth for heaven, as in the willingness to live the life of heaven here on earth.

  -Andrew Murray

******

Farewell, vain world; my soul can bid Adieu:
My Saviour's taught me to abandon you.
Your charms may gratify a sensual mind;
Not please a soul wholly for God design'd.
Forbear to entice, cease then my soul to call:
'Tis fix'd through grace; my God shall be my ALL.
While He thus lets me heavenly glories view,
Your beauties fade, my heart's no room for you.

-David Brainerd
(LDD, pg. 82)

- We must never be astonished at temptations however outrageous they may be. On this earth all is temptation. Crosses tempt us by irritating our pride, while prosperity tempts us by flattering it. Our life is a continual combat, but one in which Jesus Christ fights for us.

  -Fenelon
  (TWG, pg. 48)

Thou therefore, endure hardness, as a good soldier of Jesus Christ (2 Timothy 2:3).

- I know I long for God and a conformity to His will, in inward purity and holiness ten thousand times more than for anything here below.

  -David Brainerd
  (LDD, pg. 79)

- To let sin alone in our lives is to permit sin to grow until it chokes and blinds the conscience. Not to conquer sin is to be conquered by sin.

  -Unknown

- People are like sheep. They can be easily influenced and led astray by a few. We see this throughout history. Even though people like to think of themselves as independent, they are afraid of the liberty to make decisions, for they want to avoid personal accountability. They want to believe that they are not easily swayed, but feed their pride with what seems like honorable causes, and they will most assuredly blindly follow a person into destruction.

  -RJK

- God taught man to make coats to cover his naked body, but the devil taught him to weave deceit to cover his naked soul. Yet the more subtle you are in concealing your sin, the more flagrantly you play the fool. There are none so shamed as the liar when found out, and you are sure to be.

  -William Gurnall
  (PDC, pg. 266)

If I had not come and spoken unto them, they had not had sin: but now they have no cloak for their sin. He that hateth me hateth my Father also (John 15:22-23).

- Saul has slain his thousands, and David his ten thousands: but Satan his millions.

  -Thomas Adams
  (PDC, pg. 267)

- When there is separation between God and His people it is because His people have decided to remember Him no more, thereby, they leave Him. God never puts His people away. However, once His people walk away from Him, they became enslaved to their own iniquity. When they sell themselves to iniquity, they become servants of wickedness.

-RJK

******

Idolatry

The one sin that you do not hear much about from the pulpits of churches is idolatry, yet this sin lies at the core of all sins. It is deceitful in the sense that every age has its particular idols. They are presented in such a way that each culture embraces them, the world philosophizes about them, false religions promote them, and man bows before them as he foolishly dances around their many erected altars of sensationalism, superstition, and hateful, indifferent fanaticism. The final fruits of such idols are the same. They are unbelief towards the real God, spiritual harlotry, and death.

Ezekiel 8 and 14 tells us that idols exist in the heart and mind. Granted, we may not physically erect some image, but the identity and importance of idols find their platform in the heart, while being exalted in the imagination of man's mind.

The most predominate idol of the heart is selfishness or self-love, while the ruling idol of the mind is pride in all of its arrogance and conceit. It is from the premise of selfishness that other idols are desired and pursued, and from the great altar of pride where they are exalted, honored, and worshipped.

Until personal idols are unmasked, people have a tendency to operate in and out of unbelief. Hebrews 4:2 tells us that it is at this point that people will give way to their idolatrous preference by failing to mix true faith towards God in the matter. In essence, they fail to choose to believe and trust Him when life does not make sense.

Real challenges and problems will arise when the God of heaven will not bow down to these people's concepts or ideas about life. Due to pride, these people will judge God as being unfair, a fable, or unloving and indifferent. It is from the altar of arrogance that the heart will give way to that which will lay all affections towards God aside, to pursue an idol that will feed the flesh, tantalize the mind, and tolerate fleshly, desirable, comfortable, and convenient worship.

All idolatry is demonically inspired, but it is man that give idols their identity. This identity is often based on how the idol makes the self-life feel about itself. Fenelon summarized this by stating that, "The origin of our trouble is that we love ourselves with a blind passion that amounts to idolatry. If we love anything beyond, it is only for our own sakes."

To address idolatry would take another book. In fact, a book has addressed this matter in an explicit manner. I would suggest you read it and study it. The book is the Word of God. Although the idols of America are not obvious as in other cultures, they are very much in place. A few examples of our idols are: money, power, education, humanist philosophies, and entertainment.

Below are a few of my excerpts from teachings and writings concerning this subject. Keep in mind, anything that becomes more important to you than God and the matters of His kingdom is idolatrous. It is for this reason that the first three commandments call for us to love God above all else, solely exalt Him to His rightful place, and always maintain a proper attitude towards Him that will always end in unadulterated worship.

- ❑ The companion of idolatry is superstition.
- ❑ God takes counsel from no one, for He possesses all knowledge and wisdom. Even in spite of God's incredible majesty, man still makes and erects his gods. Often made of earthen material, these gods are formed with mouths that do not speak, feet that cannot respond, and ears that cannot hear. At best these lifeless gods erect images in the minds of their worshipper that have no substance and are powerless and dead.
- ❑ There is idolatry in what we consider low and high places. For Israel, the low places were hidden in secret chambers of darkness that could not be seen. The high places were out in the open, but they fit naturally into the terrain. For example, these high places represented groves where worship was taking place. When we think of the heart, it points to the concept of secret chambers that cannot be

observed or seen by others. In the case of the mind, it points to idolatry in high places where such exaltation naturally fits into the terrain of our thinking process.

- God then compared Himself to idols in Isaiah 44. They are nothing more than vanity. These images come out of the normal functions of life. For example, images can be made of trees, silver, and flour. We burn a tree, buy with silver, and eat flour, yet we can make our gods out of these things! Although we give idols identity and demons give them attraction, they are void of power and life. This is how silly our idolatry is. The question is how could we prefer an idol to God? The answer is simple, we can control the reality surrounding our idols, but we cannot control God.
- God always has His remnant of people who will never bow their knees to the Baals of their ages. They may be hidden away by the darkness of slavery and poverty, but their hearts remain steadfast towards God even though they live in insane times. Like Gideon, they may be threshing behind the winepress, but their spiritual search always lead them back to the reality of the one true God. In silence they may have to cleave to the past victories of God, ponder the possibilities of God in regard to the present, and trust that regardless of the circumstances, in the end He will ultimately be exalted as the only true God of heaven and earth.
- The reason that Christians fall into the traps of idolatry is because they have not learned to wait in expectation. They have never allowed their small measure of faith to be refined while waiting upon the Lord to move. They do not want to be tested, proved, and exposed. They are hoping to skip the valleys of humiliation and the silent plateaus of waiting until God speaks or moves. As a result, they never establish depth to their faith, character in their walk, nor do they witness any fruition of God's promises.

Tell ye, and bring them near; yea, let them take counsel together: who hath declared this from ancient time? Who hath told it from that time? have not I, the LORD? And there is no God else beside me; a just God and a Saviour; there is non beside me. Look unto me, and be saved, all the ends of the earth: for I am God, and there is none else (Isaiah 45:21-22).

******

Which Jesus Do You Worship?

Satan's main goal is to get you to worship him. He does not care as to the avenue in which he receives such worship. For example, if you worship any aspect of creation, you are in essence worshipping him. If you are bowing before any images, you are worshipping him. If you are preferring and bowing before the altars of wealth, power, and prestige, you are honoring the ways of Satan.

The God of the Bible is the only One who deserves worship. We know that Satan is an enemy of God. He is in fierce competition with Him; therefore, he will use any measure, good or bad or any avenue, right or wrong, to seduce people with counterfeits, nudge with logic, prod with force, or ensnare them into bowing down to his ways. However, to worship or bow down to anything other than God is idolatry. It is a blatant affront against God, breaking His commandments and showing absolute contempt for His Word.

This brings us to Jesus Christ. He was the complete manifestation of deity in human form. We see people worshipping Him in the New Testament. The problem is that there have been many different versions presented of Him. These versions are idolatrous. In most cases they are images at best that prove to be vague and lifeless. Such images prove to be nothing more than mere concepts of man that have no dimension or power. These versions can stir the sentiment, but they never impact the spirit. They can cause great devotion, but they are powerless to save or change.

It amazes me that people can perceive Jesus to be any old Jesus they imagine Him to be. Yet, they would be insulted if those they cared for accepted an imposter to fill their place or position in their lives. No doubt they would be offended at such fickleness. Yet, they perceive that God will not be offended if they accept a counterfeit when it comes to His only begotten Son. There is only one Jesus. There may be many imitators of Him, but they are not the real Jesus. This is why the way to heaven is narrow. If you do not get Jesus right, you will be exposed as a fool on judgment day.

It is vital that we know the Jesus of the Bible. He must not be just a historical figure, nor must He remain a vague religious figure. He must become the Living Christ, the Son of God. He must become alive in our hearts. He must be real in our minds, and He must become so precious to our very souls that we can do nothing more than allow ourselves to be conformed to His very image.

The question is what Jesus do you worship? Resolve this matter before you enter into the corridors of eternity, and find out that the Jesus you lay claim to was an imposter, incapable of saving you from the wrath of God.

Then if any man shall say unto you, Lo, here is Christ, or there; believe it not. For there shall arise false Christs, and false prophets, and shall show great signs and wonders; insomuch that, if it were possible, they shall deceive the very elect. Behold, I have told you before (Matthew 24:23-25).

Bits and Pieces

- Greatness is difficult to appreciate from close up. The great mountain on the horizon is only the ground when you are standing on it.

  -Unknown

- Arguing with a stubborn person is much like mud wrestling with a pig. Pretty soon you realize the pig likes it.

  -Author Unknown

- The future has many names: for the fearful it's the unknown, for the reckless it's the adventure, for the pessimists it's the unattainable. For the brave, it is opportunity.

  -Unknown

- It is all very well to be impressed with the contributions to human happiness that are made by world's leaders—the great men and women—the five-talent people who do things do them well and who usually get the notice, the publicity, the praise, and the rewards. But what we are all inclined to forget is the fact that behind them are unnumbered hosts of ordinary men and women whose names are never printed, whose faces are never captured by the newsreel cameras but whose quiet unassuming labor makes the work of the leaders possible.

  -Peter Marshall
  (JMM, pgs. 56, 57)

❖ We don't want a thing because we have found a reason for it—we find a reason for it because we want it.

-Unknown

❖ The more the people of a society lose their individuality and become like sheep, the more the leadership is infiltrated by wolves.

-Judge Andrew Napolitano

❖ Men don't follow titles, they follow courage, and if you would just lead them, they would follow you forever, and so would I.

-Braveheart

And he saith unto them, Follow me, and I will make you fishers of men (Matthew 4:19).

******

Yiddish Proverbs and Other Jewish Witticisms

- The wise man, even when he holds his tongue, says more than the fool when he speaks.
- What you don't see with your eyes, don't invent with your mouth.
- A hero is someone who can keep his mouth shut when he is right.
- One old friend is better than two new ones.
- One of life's greatest mysteries is how the boy who wasn't good enough to marry your daughter can be the father of the smartest grandchild in the world.
- Old friends, like old wines, don't lose their flavor.
- You can't control the wind, but you can adjust your sails.
- A wise man hears one word and understands two.

***

- Don't be so humble - you are not that great.

-Golda Meir
(1898-1978) to a visiting diplomat

Sayings from Albert Einstein

- Any intelligent fool can make things bigger and more complex. It takes a touch of genius - and a lot of courage to move in the opposite direction.
- Life is like riding a bicycle. To keep your balance, you must keep moving.
- When his wife asked him to change clothes to meet the German Ambassador, he said, "If they want to see me, here I am. If they want to see my clothes, open my closet and show them my suits."
- Intellectuals solve problems; geniuses prevent them.
- Not everything that counts can be counted, and not everything that can be counted counts.
- We can't solve problems by using the same kind of thinking we used when we created them.
- Education is what remains after one has forgotten everything he learned in school.
- Two things are infinite: the universe and human stupidity; and I'm not sure about the universe.

***

- Imagination is more important than knowledge.

-Sign hanging in Einstein's office at Princeton

******

Setting the Record Straight

It is not unusual to pick up some erroneous teachings along the way. Some of these teachings will not have any real effect on a person's attitude towards the matters of God, while others can produce ungodly responses.

This reminds me of two such teachings. The first one has to do with an Old Testament teaching surrounding Leviticus 16. I was taught that when the High Priest went into the Most Holy Place on the Day of Atonement to sprinkle the blood of the sacrifice on the Ark of the Covenant, that a rope was tied around his ankle. If those in the Holy

Place did not hear the bells ringing that were located on his outer robe that they would presume that he was struck dead by God.

When I shared this teaching with a Hebrew teacher, she was appalled at it. She informed me that Leviticus 16:4 states that the High Priest entered into the Most Holy Place in his white holy undergarments. In other words, the outer garment with the bells was taken off before entering the Most Holy Place to fulfill the required obligations in regard to making atonement for Israel.

Although the concept of the teaching about the rope seemed logical enough, the rope was never mentioned in Scripture. The fact that the High Priest was to observe stringent rules in regard to personal preparation before entering the Most Holy Place implied that any personal deviation would be covered by the sacrifices that he was required to make on his behalf.

The bells on the outer robe actually represented God's voice, while the white linen garments represented righteousness. Making atonement was a serious, sober time, implying that silence would be the protocol towards such a grave matter. Therefore, neither God nor man would be speaking.

According to the information I have read about the white linen, the priest would not sweat in it. We know that all righteousness finds its source and approval in God. Man could not stand righteous before the Lord on his own merit. Therefore, righteousness is imputed to man, implying that there would be no sweat on man's part to earn God's approval. He must simply be in compliance with the requirements.

The second erroneous teaching has to do with Matthew 11:12, which states, "And from the days of John the Baptist until now the kingdom of heaven suffereth violence, and the violent take it by force." Since most of Christendom does not understand the inspiration behind this Scripture, they take it literally. In spite of other Scriptures that teach to the contrary, these individuals interpret this Scripture to mean that they must use violence to further the kingdom of God.

According to the book, *Understanding the Difficult Words of Jesus,* authors David Bivin and Roy B. Blizzard explain that this Scripture is an idiom. An idiom is a saying or expression in the usage of a language that is peculiar to itself. Americans use many idioms like, "He lost his head" or "Eat your heart out." To take such sayings or expressions as being literal, would totally change the intent or impact of them.

The correct meaning to the idiom found in Matthew 11:12 can be found in an old rabbinic interpretation of Micah 2:13. It is a picture of a flock of sheep breaking forth after being penned up all night. At night, the shepherd would build a makeshift enclosure for the sheep against a hillside. In order to keep the sheep in, the shepherd would make a small breach in the fence, but he himself would lay across this "door". In the morning the sheep would be eager to get out to the pasture. Therefore, they pushed and shoved to get out, which caused a bigger breach in the wall. Jesus was basically saying that John the Baptist had marked the beginning of the kingdom of heaven breaking forth as every person who had been restrained by some type of bondage was breaking out of the different pens of the world and religion in order to follow the true Shepherd and King into the abundance of God's will, life, and purpose.

According to Bivin and Blizzard other idiomatic expressions can be found in Luke 12:49-50; 18:25; and 23:31. Obviously, to properly handle the Word of God, we either must ensure the record being presented is correct, or we must set the record straight for not only our sake, but for the sake of others.

*****

Holidays

My Favorite Holiday

Today there are those in leadership positions who are trying to change our traditions. Granted, many of our traditions or celebrations have been hijacked by commercialism. Therefore, it is clear that we need to come back to the simple intent of each holiday to properly celebrate it.

Each Jewish celebration was designed to remind the people of Israel of God's abiding intervention in their lives. It was a time for them as a collective group to celebrate the life God had given them, while recognizing that He was the author of all life. Clearly, their relationship with Him would determine the quality of their lives.

Celebrations that lack any real intent or purpose to bring into focus what needs to be important to us as individuals and as a collective group of people are not real holidays. Therefore, we need to step back from the celebration and consider what we are recognizing as being important to us.

This brings me to my favorite holiday. It is true I appreciate all the holidays. For example, I value the 4th of July because it reminds me that true freedom comes with a great cost. In fact, I am reminded of the words delivered in a sermon to the Massachusetts House of Representatives, May 26, 1773, by Pastor Charles Turner. He stated that while the people had a duty to obey good rulers, it was as much their duty to oppose destructive ones. He went on to say, "How distressing the thought of being slaves, how charming that of being free! While liberty is fruitful, in trade, industry, wealth, learning, religion and noblest virtue, all that is great and good and happy; slavery clogs every sublime movement of the soul, prevents everything excellent, and introduces poverty, ignorance, vice and universal misery among people." Sadly, Americans are beginning to feel the claws of slavery grip their very beings due to the reproach brought on us by the various abuses of abundance, ignorance of our history, and ingratitude towards true freedom. This reproach has escalated due to the presence of wicked leaders who have no moral, spiritual, or decent compass in which to test their despotic ideology. Such ideology can only create fools who do not have a shred of wisdom to foresee the consequences that will follow their wicked decisions.

Admittedly, I get caught up with the spirit of Christmas. It is a time in which great tenderness sweeps my soul as I remember how my Lord lowered Himself to accept a body prepared for Him to become a sacrificial Lamb.

Christmas always leads me to Easter or what I refer to as "Resurrection Sunday." My soul rejoices as my spirit soars over the glorious reality that a grave could not keep my Lord. We serve a risen, victorious Lord and Savior, not a lifeless martyr that is incapable of saving us.

However, my most favorite holiday is Thanksgiving. It appears that the other holidays are shrouded in controversy or made obscure by the actual celebration. As a result, the intent has been greatly thwarted. For example, there are many debates about the validity of Christ being born on December 25th, as well as the fact, that much of the celebration and concepts of Christmas find their practices in paganism. As to whether Jesus was born on December 25, there are those who would agree that He was probably born in the fall, but some cultures count the time a child was conceived as their birthday. If Jesus was born in the fall, He could have been miraculously conceived in the womb of Mary in December. However, it is not the date we are to celebrate, but the fact that God made an entrance into history in order to save mankind.

Like Christmas, the image of a bunny rabbit representing Easter proves to be more acceptable to a worldly worldview than an old rugged cross and an empty tomb. Granted, the bunny is pagan and has no place or competition with Jesus paying the price of redemption, but it is up to each of us to keep a matter pure in context and intent.

It is for this reason that I so appreciate Thanksgiving. Granted, the present presentations of those discovering America are dressed as Puritans, rather than like the pleasant Pilgrims who ventured the stormy Atlantic Ocean for two months to find freedom from oppressive religious tyranny, but the blessed intent remains the same.

Thanksgiving is a time to remember that those fleeing religious oppression came to this country as spiritual Pilgrims. They risked it all to freely worship their Creator as their conscience so dictated. They paid dearly for such freedom. When they arrived, it was winter and they were not prepared to face it. Before spring nearly half of them had died.

If was in this environment that an Indian by the name of Samoset approached them and greeted them in their own language. Apparently, he had learned their language from fishermen and traders. They believed the meeting to be a miracle, a blessing from God. A week later he returned with Squanto, who lived with the Pilgrims and accepted their Christian faith.

It was after much prayer and the help of the Indians that the Pilgrims were able to reap a bountiful harvest. It was because of the blessings of God that the Pilgrims declared a three-day feast in December 1621 to thank God and to celebrate with their Indian friends. This was the seed that would spring into fruits from generation to generation, defining our present-day celebration of Thanksgiving.

Notice that I stated that this was the seed of thankfulness that produced fruit. Due to God's clear blessing and abiding intervention on behalf of the people of this new country, the example and practices of Thanksgiving were recognized and observed by the New England Colonies. The people recognized their need for God, and would set a day apart for prayer and fasting in the spring and a day of prayer and thanksgiving in the fall. This practice began to spread southward until the American Revolution. During this time Congress issued seven separate proclamations for times of fasting and prayer, for only God would be able to see an infant country come to maturity.

American's first national Thanksgiving occurred in 1789 with the commencement of the Federal Government. It was noted by Mr. Elias Boudinot that he could not think of letting the session pass without offering an opportunity to all the citizens of the United States of joining in one voice in returning to Almighty God their sincere thanks for the many blessings He had poured down upon them. President George Washington heartily concurred with the request and issued the first federal Thanksgiving proclamation.

That same year the Episcopal Church that President Washington was a member of announced that the first Thursday in November would become its regular day for giving thanks to God for His blessings, unless otherwise appointed by civil authorities.

When you study the information about Thanksgiving that the *Wall Builders* provide through their website, you will see where well-known Congressmen and Governors declared a day of Thanksgiving for the country, the state, and the communities. Names such as Samuel Adams, Richard Henry Lee, Thomas Jefferson, and John Hancock were identified to such declarations.

However, much of the credit for the adoption of Thanksgiving as an annual national holiday can be attributed to Mrs. Sarah Josepha Hale. She was the editor of popular lady's books, *Godey's Lady's Book.* She promoted the concept of Thanksgiving for three decades, ending with her contacting President Abraham Lincoln. The president responded by setting aside the last Thursday of that November.

It must be noted that President Lincoln's proclamation was greatly influenced by the backdrop of the Civil War. It was issued during the darkest days of the conflict. The Union had lost battle after battle throughout the first three years. Yet, Lincoln called upon Americans to pray with an air of positive optimism and genuine thankfulness.

The Thanksgiving Proclamation came at a pivotal point of Lincoln's spiritual life. Just three months prior, he had to face the carnage of war at Gettysburg. It had cost 60,000 American lives. It was while Lincoln was walking among the thousands of graves that he first committed his life to Christ. He later explained to a clergyman: "When I left Springfield (Illinois, to assume the Presidency), I asked the people to pray for me. I was not a Christian. When I buried my son, the severest trial of my life, I was not a Christian. But when I went to Gettysburg and saw the graves of thousands of our soldiers, I then and there consecrated myself to Christ."

Over seventy-five years the presidents followed Lincoln's Thanksgiving Proclamation. Due to the sporadic changes surrounding celebrating Thanksgiving on the last Thursday in November, President Franklin D. Roosevelt set the fourth Thursday apart of each November to celebrate this auspicious celebration. It was in 1941 that Congress permanently established the fourth Thursday as Thanksgiving.

Even though Thanksgiving is being presently attacked, it is what it is. Individually and as a nation it reminds us that when we consider all we have, we cannot thank the government for such blessings because it cannot produce them. In fact, it must rely on the blessings of the people to even function. We cannot offer thanksgiving to others for they are simply instruments in which blessings are imparted to and through. Clearly, they have no means to multiply them. And, if we perceive that we have earned or acquired what we have without any real intervention on God's part, we will see no need to be thankful, because there would be no blessing in it.

I, for one, am glad there is One whom I can thank for my many blessings. If I thought the blessings came from an indifferent, oppressive government, I would fall into complete despair over what would amount to nothing more than crumbs. If I thought the blessings depended on the fickle sentiments of people, I would have to fight disillusionment because such blessings would be a mixed bag of unpredictability and self-serving kindness. And, if I concluded that I was the source of my blessing, I would count myself as being a most miserable, ungrateful wretch.

As decent, God-fearing people we must always remember that blessings are given by a God who is full of mercy, grace, and love. All that we have is a matter of His grace, the goodness we experience is because of His love, and the kindness we taste is because of His mercy. Let us truly bring Him back to center focus and praise Him for His goodness, thank Him for His grace, bless Him for His faithfulness, honor Him for His greatness, and worship Him in His glory.

******

- How proper it is that Christmas should follow Advent. –For him who looks toward the future, the Manger is situated on Golgotha, and the Cross has already been raised in Bethlehem.

  -Dag Hammarskjold
  (HFG, pg. 189)

For to me to live is Christ, and to die is gain (Philippians 1:21).

- We are entering upon a new year, we shall have
  new toils,
  new trials,
  new temptations, and
  new troubles.
  In whatever state, in whatever place, into whatever condition we may be brought this year--let us seek grace to follow our Lord's loving advice, and "look up!"

  -James Smith

And when these things begin to come to pass, then look up, and lift up your heads; for your redemption draweth nigh (Luke 21:28).

Just for Fun

Hidden Names

In the short story below are the names of 34 people who are recorded in the Bible. Some of these names are obvious, but others are found in words, while some are separated by a space or some type of punctuation such as a comma or period. Some names are well known, while others are not. See how acquainted you are with the people of the Bible by how many names you are able to find in the paragraph below. If you are not sure, you can always take a peek at the names on page 248, and see if you can actually locate them before looking at their unveiling in the story. Perhaps you might note some similarities between the characters in this story and the people of the Bible, as well as recognize fundamental Biblical truths.

***

A man named John had various abandoned creatures he cared for at a farm outside of an unincorporated place called Pauley, located in Jameson County. In the beginning the various animals kept everything in somewhat of a chaotic state; therefore, he called the place Babel. However, in time he had developed procedures that made a lot of improvements, as well as eliminated many challenges. As a result, he felt accomplished in his job. Even his wife, Ada videoed the various measures they both had instituted to help the place to run smoothly. It was obvious to any onlooker that they made mass improvements. It was so fined-tuned that Ada made special food for exotic creatures such as their snake, Lulu and a mouthy parrot named Simon to save money and ensure their health. Clearly, the couple had added to the quality of the lives of the creatures entrusted to their care. However, on this particular day, John had an ominous feeling. Unknowingly, it would be a day he would mark down in his journal as being insightful. Like always, he took the time to clean and hose all the different cages of the creatures entrusted to him. He also took note that at least the orphaned cats, Zacchaeus was comfortably resting on his normal perch, and Joshua had once again secured his preferred place on the old chair. As he absent-mindedly leaned down to pet, Ernest, his dog, he became aware of a stir in the barn. A brash incident was clearly occurring. He rushed to the scene to see with consternation that his snake was on the loose. Usually, the snake, Lulu, kept low key, but at other times her odd and unpredictable mannerisms made her a Judas. This time her activities appeared as if she was causing a major danger to the order of the facility. She had somehow slipped out of her glass case and was making an assault on the cage of the rabbit, Maryjo. From John's immediate summation of the situation, it was obvious that a most interesting set of events were quickly being set into motion. The snake was actually attempting to wrap herself around the cage of the anxious rabbit. Clearly, Maryjo abhorred Lulu seeing her as a possible meal. Even though the wire of her cage kept her protected from the assault, it ushered panic into the midst of the barn. Maryjo's excited state was causing the hamster, Dorcus to spin her wheel out of control in her cage, causing her cage to fall off of the table. The sound of the cage inspired the squirrel, Nimrod to burrow a hole in the straw, and the skunk, Cain, to turn his posterior to the whole fiasco. Since the snake was trying to put the squeeze on the rabbit, the raccoon, Ahab was taking the opportunity to eye the goldfish, Basil as it was swimming in a make-shift pond near by. Before he could save Maryjo, resurrect Dorcus' cage, uncover Nimrod from his hiding place, turn Cain in the right direction, remove Ahab from temptation, and pull Basil out of the possible jaws of death, John had to subdue the instigator behind the chaos. As he unwrapped Lulu from the cage, he began to wonder about his procedures. If one snake can throw everything into chaos in a matter of seconds, what does it say about the real plans and intelligence of mankind? Perhaps our first parents in the Garden of Eden could easily answer that question.

(To see if you located all of the names in the puzzle, see pages 248-249.)

Treasures of the Heart

The following stories are either incidents I was personally involved in or stories that I have heard or read. Once again, details can prove to be fuzzy, but the impact these incidents and stories made in my life are powerful.

It is my hope that they will make an impact on your life as well.

A Child Will Lead:

The Lord used children as an example. It is for this reason we are told that there will be times when children will lead adults. I heard of two different stories about children that greatly impacted my life. In a way it helped me redefine what I valued and thought to be important.

The first story was about a Korean boy. I cannot remember his exact age, but he believed on the Lord Jesus. He had a sincere, but firm belief in what was accomplished by Jesus on the cross on his behalf. When the Communists invaded Korea, they came to this young boy's community and called for all the Christians to come to the church building. Since he was a believer, he naturally responded to their call.

When the Christians were gathered together, the Communist soldiers lined each of them up against the wall of the sanctuary. They put a pistol to each person's head and demanded that each one renounce his or her faith in Christ. Sadly, under the threat of death each person renounced their faith in Christ, that is until the soldiers came to the young boy. When they commanded the boy to renounce his faith, he refused. They continued to badger him with threats of death and punishment, but each time he became more resolved in his faith. He told them there was no way he could deny his Lord because of what He had done for him.

Out of frustration, the soldiers took him into a room and tried to use separation as a means of persuasion and coercion into verbally making him denounce his faith, but he would not recant his declarations about Jesus.

The soldiers could see the young boy would not budge. They took him back to the sanctuary. As he stood there waiting for the inevitable to happen, the soldiers took their guns and killed every person standing in the church, except the boy. The boy was shocked. He asked the soldiers why they had killed those who denied their faith, while keeping him alive after he refused to deny his Lord.

They admitted to him that those who are quick to deny their faith would not prove to be faithful to the cause of Communism. However, if they could convince him that their ideology was correct, they had no doubt that he would be the best Communist he could be. The saying, "If you fail to stand for anything, you will end up falling for everything," is indeed true.

Did the Communists convince this young man that his faith was foolish and vain? According to the story, this young man became a powerful evangelist. It was clear that he never moved from the immovable Rock of ages, the Lord Jesus Christ.

The other story that I heard took place in China. The Chinese found themselves in great conflict against oppressive and cruel rebels. One of the targets of the oppressive conflict became Christian institutions. One day rebels came to a Christian school. They made a crude cross and placed it in front of the gate of the school. They told the students that if they did not trample the cross down, they would never make it home alive.

The first four teenage boys that were released ran over the cross. The cross was once again set up in front of the gate. The next person to exit the door of the school was an eight-year-old girl. As she came up to the cross, she kneeled before it. True to their word, they executed her. This young martyr may have not have made it to her physical home, but she was welcomed to her new home in glory. When she opened her eyes, she was met with the unfolding glory of heaven as she looked into the wonderful face of Jesus.

The question was how would the rest of the students respond to the cross in light of this young girl's martyrdom? Apparently, every student after her followed her example. Likewise, they entered into glory and would also be named among the faithful martyrs of the past as they forever bathed in the abiding presence and glory of their Lord and Savior.

But Jesus said, Suffer little children, and forbid them not, to come unto me: for of such is the kingdom of heaven (Matthew 19:14).

A Mother's Commitment:

We often remember the greatness of men, but how much do we ponder the influence and impact of godly women? How many great men have been influenced by humble, meek mothers, sisters, or wives? We know about the faith of Moses' mother, the leadership of Deborah, the desperate heart of Hannah, and the purity of a handmaiden named, Mary. We also know that the Apostle Paul reminded Timothy about the unfeigned faith of the influential women of his life.

If there was a hall of frame for women of God, the woman I am about to write about would be honored in it. Hidden away by the giant shadows cast by two of her sons, there was nothing unassuming or insignificant in the role she had in her children's lives.

One of the events that clearly shaped her life was the destruction of her home by fire. Some would consider what was noteworthy of such an event besides possible physical loss that would impact her so much. However, there was a precious treasure in the house that could not be restored. It was her six-year-old son.

The house was so engulfed by flames that any rescue of her child seemed impossible. Granted, she had eight children, but none could be replaced for they were all precious. Her scream was silent and her heart breaking as her husband knelt on the ground and committed their son to the capable hands of God. When all hope seemed to perish in the flames, she spotted her son in a window. As she struggled to grasp the reality of the situation, a neighbor ran through the scorching heat and pulled him to safety just seconds before the burning roof collapsed.

Some of you are probably rejoicing at the miracle of it all. However, there is something you need to know. The name of the mother was Susanna, and the son that was saved that night was John Wesley, the founder of the Methodist Church.

We must consider the mother of John Wesley, for her character, example, and commitment resonated through his life. She was acquainted with hardship and sorrow. She was the youngest in a family of 25 children. She, herself, bore 19 children of which only nine lived to adulthood. Susanna struggled to provide for her family, especially when her pastor husband spent time in prison for mishandling financial funds. Her only livelihood of diary cows were also wiped out after one of her husband's enemies slaughtered them during the night.

Susanna's main goal was to raise her children in the ways of the Lord. Since she recognized that God had his hand on her fifteenth child, John, she was determined to spend extra hours instilling the truths of God's kingdom into her children. She set two hours aside for her relationship with the Lord, but spent six hours daily for twenty years teaching her children. She also conducted Sunday night service in her home that grew to 200 people.

As we consider the life of Susanna Wesley, we must realize that without her there would never have been a John or Charles Wesley. (TB, pgs 251-257).

When I call to remembrance the unfeigned faith that is in thee, which dwelt first in thy grandmother, Lois, and thy mother, Eunice; and I am persuaded that in thee also (2 Timothy 1:5).

You Owe....

The direction of Gentle Shepherd Ministries was changing. We had a nice two passenger pickup but we knew that we needed a different vehicle because other people would be involved in the promotion of our ministry as well.

One of our teammates had a cousin who was a car salesman. We knew that to secure a decent car on a trade in and with very little money would require a miracle. However, we knew that our God was more than capable of securing what we needed, and it was clear that circumstances were requiring us to step out in faith.

Unbeknown to me before we went to the car lot, the Lord impressed upon Jeannette to be open-minded to consider a foreign model. Jeannette was a strong advocate in buying American made products, especially vehicles.

We felt we needed a van, but when we considered how much even a used van would cost, we knew it was out of the question. As we discussed our options with the car dealer, he asked if we would be interested in a used station wagon. After all, it would fit our criteria. He told us that he had two models. One was a Ford and the other one a Nissan.

When we walked towards the two cars, it was obvious the Ford was well used. However, the Nissan was in great shape. The salesman told us the difference between the two vehicles and suggested that based on their condition, the Nissan would probably serve us well.

Remembering what the Lord had already impressed upon her, Jeannette was willing to test drive the Nissan. However, we were met with a bit of an obstacle. Someone had locked the keys in the station wagon. They had to break in. As they were breaking in, the car's alarm was tripped. The horn began to beep and the lights were flashing in utter protest. Jeannette saw the car as having a personality, which somewhat endeared her to it on an emotional level.

The minute she got into the driver's seat she felt as if the car had been designated just for her. She loved the design of the seat and how it felt on the open road. When we arrived at the lot, we both knew that we wanted the car. However, the issue of money could very well thwart any hopes of purchasing it.

The salesman went in to figure out how much we would owe after the trade in of the pickup. We knew that a Nissan had a higher resale value than our Ford pickup would, but we also knew we had to give something for God to work with.

As we waited for the news, Jeannette told me the Lord had given her the difference we were to pay for a car. When I asked her the total, I have to admit when she told me the amount, I knew that it would take a miracle to get the car. The amount she was given was a whopping $20.00. Obviously, if we walked away with the car it would be a "God-thing".

After about 20 minutes the salesman came out with the paperwork. He looked at us with a serious expression on his face. He told us after figuring out everything including the sales tax, that in order to walk away with the car we owed the dealership—fourteen dollars and seventy-seven cents.

Watch ye, stand fast in the faith, quit you like men, be strong (1 Corinthians 16:13).

How Far Will God Reach?

We sometimes forget how far God will go to reach His lost sheep. We know that He gave up the glories of heaven and came to earth. We think it is quite noble of Him to do such a feat, but we really have no consensus as to the heights He came down from in order to secure our salvation. It truly shows a love that is unfathomable and a sacrifice that could never be measured. And to think, He did it so He could offer the gift of life to each of us that is priceless and complete.

God's reaching into the midst of grave darkness and depravity did not stop with the death, burial, and resurrection of Jesus Christ. He continues to reach down from the heights of heaven to reach people in the great depths of darkness.

This reality became even more poignant in the case of our friend Amy (named has been changed). Because of a mutual acquaintance, Amy had contacted us through the internet. She admitted that she had been in a commune for 26 years that was anti-God and anti-Jesus. The leadership had used fear to control and hate to compel. After being in touch with our mutual acquaintance she had been moved by tears. For the first time she sensed life because of what was said about God in their conversation. She wanted materials to help her come to terms with God, as well as the Christian life. Our mutual friend directed her our way.

We realize that it took a lot for Amy to contact us. We were not about to let the door shut on such a tender seeking soul. I have to admit, we had no idea what we would find on the other side of the door, but we could see the desperation in her life. To make a long story short, the actual commune Amy came out of was hardcore witchcraft. She not only worshipped Satan for 26 years in different covens, she had climbed up the ranks to where she taught new aspiring converts to secure the most powerful spirit guide.

Through our e-mail communications with Amy, she began to open up more and more. She admitted that she had sought out the Christian life by attending different churches for over twelve years. However, most bodies ignored her, and for those who knew who she was, she was told to come late and leave early. Sadly, none of these shepherds or bodies reached out to her. She eventually gave up seeking and settled for a miserable existence of fear, torment, and uncertainty.

As the nightmarish truth came out about her life, I could not help but ask her how in the world she ever escaped the far-reaching tentacles of the kingdom of darkness. People do not leave covens unless it is feet first. And, after being rejected by Christians, why had she never given up on finding the real answers about God? What she shared with me so impacted me that I felt it could not remain hidden. As believers, such stories remind us why God deserves to be sanctified in our hearts and glorified in our lives.

One day, when Amy was sitting in a candle-lit room chanting to Satan, a beam of light came from the joint connecting the ceiling and wall and penetrated right into her heart flooding her with God's love. She looked to the person next to her and asked if she could see the light. However, it became obvious that only Amy was seeing and experiencing the phenomena. Then a Voice spoke to her. It said two words, "You're leaving!"

Amy did not know how she would escape, but the opportunity presented itself when she received permission to attend her relative's wedding. Even though she was tormented and an actual attempt was made by the coven to take her life, God protected her and thwarted such plans.

As we waded through her fears and questions, the wrestling match over her soul proved to be intense. I had no idea what truth, hope, or promise the Holy Spirit would use to penetrate her inner being to bring resolution to her spirit in regard to her spiritual search for salvation. One day, when we were talking on the phone, we came upon the very subject that would serve as a light of hope. The subject was heaven.

During the conversation, I asked Amy as a dedicated follower of Satan where she planned to spend eternity. She told me that followers of Satan were promised a room in hell where they would actually be able to rest. After all, these poor people were continually tormented by their demonic companions. They have no peace or rest.

When I heard about the false promise of the kingdom of darkness, I immediately told her that Satan was lying to her. Hell was not a place of rest, but of utter torment. What she desired was heaven. I proceeded to take her through Scriptures about both places. After we were done with our study, Amy admitted that she did not want to spend eternity in hell, but in heaven. It was from that point that Amy began to open her heart up to the Lord Jesus Christ.

Not surprising, the first extensive study Amy did as a new convert was on New Jerusalem, which represents heaven coming down to earth. She sent the study to us. I want to share some of her findings with you:

Description of the city: Divine architect. Its description is beyond imagination. It is celestial in origin, and no mortal hands were employed in its construction. It will be suspended above the new earth.

Size: Everything in it is in multiples of twelve. It is 1500 square miles. Its height and breath are equal. It could be a pyramid in shape. Width wise it would reach from Maine to Florida, or California to Oklahoma.

Wall: The wall of jasper is massive and high. The outer circumference would be 6,000 lineal miles long and 212' to 216' thick.

Foundations: Twelve foundations made of different precious stone. These beautiful foundations remind us of God's faithfulness to keep His promises. The twelve foundations have the twelve names of the apostles on them. This reminds us of the sure foundation that ensures a perfect government.

Gates: There are twelve gates, three on each side of the city. At each gate is an angel. They had the twelve tribes of Israel written on them, and are fifty miles wide and are made of a single pearl. They remind us that the only way of salvation came by way of the Jews and that they will never be closed because of God's great work of redemption.

Streets: If there was a street running through the city from each gate, there would be a grid of sixteen squares—each square would have 18 million acres. That would be 625 million of our city blocks. Running N & S: If you consider one street per mile for 1500 miles, with each street being 1500 miles long would equal 2,250,000 miles of street. Running E & W: there would be an equal amount of streets of 2,250,000 which would equal a total of 4,500,000 miles of streets in New Jerusalem. If you drove at 25 MPH it would take 180,000 hours to see New Jerusalem.

Since no sleep is required, at 24 hours a day it would take 7,500 days to tour the first floor, or at 365 days a year, it would take 20.5 years for the 1st floor. (It is good thing we will have our new bodies.)

However, the city is 1500 miles high. Therefore, at one floor/level per mile = 1500 levels high, it would give us 67,500,000 miles of streets. You could see all of it in a mere 307.5 years if you do nothing more than tour it 24 hours a day, 365 days a year, traveling at the slow speed of 25 MPH.

Since we have eternity to explore this incredible place, we could take our time. Therefore, if you travel only 8 hours a day at 25 MPH, the first level would take 61.6 years. The 15 levels would take a mere 924 years.

Amy ended her study by stating that there will be no mortuaries, deaths, funerals, or graves, along with jails, hospitals, sickness, or tears. These were important facts to her because Amy knew all about death, despair, and tears.

The thing that amazes me is that Amy had no problem believing God existed, since He was a true enemy of Satan. She did not question that there was a heaven or hell. She knew she was destined for hell, but what she desired was peace in light of the torment she had endured. She did not argue with the Voice that had spoke to her that day because the coven had taught her to obey without question. She did not debate what the Bible said because she knew it was true.

We Christians take much for granted. We often live in the gray area where matters are neither light nor darkness, right or wrong, just or unjust. But, for Amy there is no gray area. She knows the distinction between light and darkness.

Amy is a remarkable woman. When she was first set free from her spirit guide, she sang Gospel hymns with true purity. In spite of all she witnessed, her giggle is innocent as a child's and the simple ways in which she approaches the matters of life and eternity reminds me of what the Apostle Paul said in 2 Corinthians 11:3. He was concerned that our minds would be corrupted from the simplicity that is in Christ. In Amy's case, Satan and his ways of darkness clearly drove her to seek out and discover the simplicity found in the light of the world and the hope of heaven, Jesus Christ.

Looking for and hasting unto the coming of the day of God, wherein the heavens being on fire shall be dissolved, and the elements shall melt with fervent heat? Nevertheless, we, according to his promise, look for new heavens and a new earth, wherein dwelleth righteousness (2 Peter 3:12-13).

The Unlikely:

When we think of heroes, we have a tendency to think of those who have been somewhat immortalized by the world of fantasy, literature, media sources, and comic books such as Superman. Such heroes only live in the imaginations of those who have taken a fancy to them.

Why is it at this time of history that we must make heroes and heroines into unrealistic veggie tales or into ruthless fornicators who lack real decency or morals? Have we fallen so low in our moral caliber that we do not desire the substance of character more than a temporary moment of sentiment that comes out of fantasy? Do we desire truth more than delusion?

It is for this reason that I have discovered that there can be no courage unless there is character. There have been unlikely individuals who have raised a standard of excellence. The reason for raising such a standard was not a matter of honor or choice, but one of necessity. Each time people have considered the standard these individuals raised, they have to pause and label such an individual as being courageous. After all, they often had to go against the acceptable tides of their times.

Have you ever heard of a man named Columba? He lived during the sixth century. He was a dichotomy for he was known as a saint and fighter. He had a passion for God, but he also possessed an explosive temper. This temper served as a platform for his anger. Although he had ties with the Lord of heaven, his anger could erupt at any time towards those who dared oppose him. His explosive temper robbed him of his credibility as a believer.

One such person who opposed him was the king. Columba's anger seethed against him. Eventually it erupted into a confrontation that cost the lives of 5,000 men. The death of these men brought him to a place of real humility and repentance. As a result, the weight of the senseless deaths of these men caused by his anger was put aside as the Lord bathed him in His forgiveness.

Due to learning his lesson, Columba's next encounter with a king led to the king's salvation. And, as for the 5,000 souls who were lost due to his anger, many more than 5,000 souls were added to the rolls of heaven because of the godly man he became. (TB, pgs. 114-117)

Courage requires us to first face our inner character. It produces the type of state that will humble a person enough that heaven will end up honoring him or her.

Have you ever heard or read about the man who did not want to be pope? He lived in the sixth century and died in the seventh century. This godly man actually fled the monastery to avoid being chosen as the head of the Church. He had to be hunted down and escorted to the place where he would be ordained as pope.

Instead of relishing his position, this man despised what he called "celestial justice" that punished those who dared to oppose the papacy. This man knew that "no repentance" takes place under the scourge of religious tyranny. He even raged against the titles men bestowed upon him. He was repulsed at the concept of being considered the "universal pope." He felt such usurpation was a foolish, proud assumption that was profane, wicked, blasphemous, and diabolical. In his mind it rated up there with the arrogance of Lucifer. The title he desired was simple, but it spoke of his inner character and attitude towards God. He instructed others to call him, "the servant".

Succeeding popes tried to capture a bit of this man's reputation, only to show themselves to be more arrogant and unreasonable in their claims and actions. Some leaders even falsely dismissed this man's attitude as being conceited arrogance. Yet, this man was anything but conceited and arrogant. He was in the truest sense a simple servant of the Most High God. In his position, he never forgot the need to maintain and preserve his inner character.

This man rightfully possessed the title he so deserved. As our Lord stated, those who desire to be great in His kingdom must become a servant of all. This man became known as Gregory the Great. (TB, pgs. 122-126)

But it shall not be so among you: but whosoever will be great among you, let him be your minister; And whosoever will be chief among you, let him be your servant (Matthew 20:26-27).

The Hymnal:

My co-laborer in the Gospel, Jeannette, held the old hymnal in her hands. Recognizing that one day the old trusted hymnals would be discarded by many as relics of the past, Jeannette started collecting them. However, the hymnal she held in her hands was elevated above the other hymnals as being significant. It was the hymnal that belonged to her great-grandmother.

Jeannette's memory of her great-grandmother consisted of her readiness to play hymns on her pump organ. It was her ministry. In fact, she would often go out and gather the rowdy neighborhood children into her small place to share Jesus with them, as well as play spiritual songs on her organ. It is hard to say the impact she made on those impressionable souls, but there is one thing for certain, she made a lasting impression on her great-granddaughter.

In her hymnal, Jeannette's great-grandmother had made certain notations alongside some of the hymns. No doubt she was signifying the importance of the message or impact they made on her life.

It is hard to watch an important part of the Church's spiritual heritage being replaced with that which lacks real substance. To read the stories about the lives of those who penned the precious hymns reveal that a high price often inspired them. In so many ways there was a simplicity to the hymns that also possessed depth that could reach into the inner soul of seeking, hurting, and wounded individuals.

For example, take the woman by the name of Charlotte Elliot. She was a carefree person who pretty well lived her life on her terms. She enjoyed the ways of the world, and took pleasure in tasting its various fruits. She was the life of the party, entertaining her friends with her humorous poetry, as well as painting or drawing their portraits.

However, her carefree lifestyle came to an abrupt end when she was 30 years of age. She found herself confined to her bed in an invalid state. The humor left as she became bitter. Needless to say, she ceased to be the life of the party or one that others sought out for companionship.

Charlotte's situation changed when Dr. Caesar Malan, a famous evangelist from Switzerland came to visit her. It was this man who penetrated her dark world of pain, suffering, anger, bitterness, and despair with the blessed hope and joy of Jesus Christ. As she struggled with how unworthy she felt in her wretched state, Malan shared how Jesus came into the world to save sinners such as her.

Charlotte embraced the message of salvation. Although she would spend 52 years of her life in bed, she would do so in light of the reality of her wondrous Lord and Savior. Even though her name would not be recognized by most, the song that she wrote after her conversion has been sung by many for the last three centuries. Perhaps you will recognize it. The song she penned was, *"Just as I am."* (TB, pgs. 295-299)

Who comforteth us in all our tribulation, that we may be able to comfort them who are in any trouble, by the comfort wherewith we ourselves are comforted of God (2 Corinthians 1:4).

Bring us our crown of life:

A missionary by the name of Boniface (AD 675-754) literally raced through Germany and the Netherlands with the saving Gospel of Jesus Christ. He was a fearless missionary who confronted the lifeless idols of the ignorant masses. He even chopped down a tree to prove to the Hessians their god was lifeless and useless. He would demolish pagan temples while building churches on the ruins of idolatrous structures. Many heard the message because of his passion, causing them to turn from their old ways to worship the true God of heaven.

At the age of 75, he was still running the race after winning Frisians to Christ and confronting the hatred and jealousy of those who were Pharaohs in heart. At the final leg of his race, he encountered those who would never concede their dark influences over the masses. As those who opposed him rushed towards Boniface and his 52 companions with murder in their hearts, he looked at his faithful co-laborers declaring, "They are coming to bring us our crown of life! Let us wait for them here." (TB, pgs. 129-131)

Henceforth there is laid up for me a crown of righteousness, which the Lord, the righteous judge, shall give me at that day: and not to me only, but unto all them also that love his appearing (2 Timothy 4:8).

The least in the kingdom of heaven:

What would it take to raise you or me out of a state of comfort to tread into areas that would shock us to the core? For a Quaker woman named Elizabeth Fry, it was reading and believing the words of Jesus in Matthew 25 that reveals what would prove to be the real test as to our spiritual character. The fruits of acceptable character would express themselves by providing basic needs for those who were victims of circumstances, as well as visiting those in prison and comforting those who are distressed.

Her obedience to the Lord's instructions brought her to the infamous Newgate Prison of London in the early 1800s. The occupants were not only foul, angry, and unmanageable, but the conditions were appalling. The women's children were also incarcerated with them. These poor waifs had no chance or opportunity to climb out of the oppression. There were no beds, sheets, or blankets. A few filthy rags served as clothing and mere scraps of food for meals. The women shoved and fought over the window gratings where they begged for a few shillings to buy liquor, their only hope for temporary escape from the abyss of hopelessness.

No doubt the scene had to be shocking to the modestly dressed Quaker woman, the mother of eight children. She had asked for this and now she was in what appeared to be a "lion's den." However, she knew that the Lord's words were not optional. She did not come to judge these poor, wretched lost souls, but to show compassion. All she could do was bring the words of life. The impact they made on these women would come down to the Lord's ability to reach into the depths of such souls with mercy and hope.

As she read the Bible in her prison surroundings for the first time, the women began to grow quiet. Even the children took note of the sweet, pure, living words of God. However, once the reading stopped, the women went back to their hellish state of fighting and utter despair.

Even though it seemed like little was being accomplished, Elizabeth could not forget her responsibility as a believer. She knew that she had to meet these poor wretched souls' basic needs to bring order, but that proved to be overwhelming. She recognized that the children, who were bound by the same prison doors as their mothers, needed to learn how to read if they were to rise above their deplorable conditions. When she informed the mothers that she was going to teach the children to read, they likewise begged her to teach them as well.

Months and years passed. Her family grew from eight children to eleven children. However, she could not ignore how God's Words and compassion were changing the lives and conditions of these women and children. She had to often scrape to provide for the basic needs of these poor souls, but God seemed to always provide. Even the prison governor who first laughed at her request was no longer laughing. The change was obvious. Upon the request of the Quaker woman, he even agreed to hire a matron to supervise the women prisoners.

John Randolph, a renowned Virginian Congressman personally witnessed the transformation taking place at Newgate Prison six years after Elizabeth's first visit. He wrote to his friend about his visit. "I saw the greatest curiosity in London! I have seen Elizabeth Fry in Newgate, and I have witnessed their miraculous effects of true Christianity upon the most depraved of human beings—bad women. Sir, who are worse, if possible, than the Devil himself. And yet the wretched outcasts have been tamed and subdued by the Christian eloquence of Mrs. Fry. Nothing but true religion can become an avenue for this miracle!"

Elizabeth's efforts would not remain in Newgate. Her call to minister to the outcast, often who were put into prisons of obscurity and death to be remembered no more, reached as far as Belgium, Holland, Prussian, Switzerland, Germany, and Australia. In France she had permission to visit any prison at any time. She corresponded with people in Italy, Denmark, and Russia who wanted to improve prisons in their countries. Her ministry also included mental institutions and hospitals in Ireland. In the end, kings and princes were asking for her recommendation in regard to prison reform. Even King Frederick William IV of Prussia asked to visit Newgate Prison with Elizabeth Fry when he was a guest of England.

After reading the Bible, she knelt with the prisoners to pray. Likewise, the king of Prussia knelt before the invisible altar. That day the cross of Jesus proved one thing, that we all stand on the same common ground before the King of kings. All of us, regardless of our status, need to be saved from a wretched state. Perhaps that which imprisons us is not obvious, but nevertheless we are all bound by some type of prison, that is, until Jesus gloriously opens the prison doors and unlock the chains that bind our hearts and minds. It is for this reason that we who possess the hope of heaven have been called to identify with those who are considered the worst of the lot with the wondrous message of promise, hope, and life. After all, in light of Jesus and His glorious redemption, we all begin at the status of being considered the least in the kingdom of God. (TB. Pgs. 285-291)

Then shall the righteous answer him, saying, Lord, when saw we thee hungred, and fed thee? or thirsty and gave thee drink? When saw we thee a stranger, and took thee in? or naked, and clothed thee? Or when saw we thee sick, or in prison, and came unto thee? And the King shall answer and say unto them, Verily I say unto you, Inasmuch as ye have done it unto one of the least of these my brethren, ye have done it unto me (Matthew 25:37-40).

The King who was:

I'm sure you might have heard stories about the escapades of various kings and queens. Although we like to think that those in such positions represent excellence, the reality is that such individuals are part of the Adamic lineage. They are prone to the wretched ways of the flesh. If they do not have moral character and decency, they will prove to be a royal pain. If these leaders are tyrannical and indifferent to the people, the oppression that will come in like a tidal wave will prove to be unbearable. Such despotic leadership not only ends in innocent people being offered up on some insane altar, but they produce revolutions that cause any decency present in civilizations to spiral downward into an abyss of death and destruction.

When you study the kings of Israel, the fruits of each king reveal much about their character. Clearly, no position can guarantee integrity of character. Goodly character will only become a natural preference when it is forged into a person in accordance to sound righteous decisions and judgments.

There are also a few Gentile kings who stand out because of their relationship to God. One such king was James 1. This particular king's first act in his royal position was to push a draft for an act of Parliament for a new version of the Bible. The purpose for such an act to be implemented was to reduce the diversities of bibles circulating throughout England. In fact, under the reign of such kings as Henry the eighth and Edward the sixth, the translations of the Bible were corrupt and not answerable to the truth of the most accepted version.

The king sought out the best biblical Scholars and linguists of that day to take on the sober task. There were 54 men nominated, but only 47 were known to have taken part in the work of translation.

Fifteen strict rules were put into place to ensure the proper translations. These rules included that the translators must refrain from alliterating from the truth from the ordinary Bible that was read by the Bishops in Church; the pronunciation and meaning of the names of prophets, writers, and books had to be preserved as much as possible; that if there was doubt, the intent and meaning had to be in line with the Founding Fathers; and there must be no marginal notes in which to influence the reader. This version was completed in 1611.

These are just a couple of examples of the strict rules, but it was clear that all possible restraints to maintain the integrity of the Word were in place. As I pondered the history of the infamous King James Version, I wondered what the king would think of the endless versions of bibles that now bombard us. To me the various versions and paraphrases do not speak of our ability to offer God's Word in a way that is understandable; rather, they cause chaos to reign in regard to truth. If you do not like one version, seek out another. I am not so sure that the various versions have not been brought forth to undermine the pure Word of God.

Today the King James Version of the Bible is under attack. This attack has nothing to do with its validity, but with its intent. It does not waiver from what constitutes sin, the Gospel, and the identity of the true God. My conclusion is if God does not intervene within a few years, it will be outlawed altogether. However, its truths will remain, and one day will judge those who do not want to love the truth of God.

Another King that made an impact on the kingdom of God was a king named Edmund. He was the king of East Anglia. This English king was crowned on Christmas day in 855 A.D. He was of the age of 14 or 15.

This young king was a godly king and served as a model of excellence. For example, he memorized the Psalms in a year and treated all with equal justice.

In 866, the Danes invaded his kingdom. Edmund struggled to defend his small state against them. He built a dike that kept them at bay for a few years. However, they gathered a larger force that could not be held.

The Danes insisted on a surrender that King Edmund could not accept as a Christian due to its pagan nature. To him, his faith was dearer to him than life. He would never dream of offending the Lord. As a result, the king sent the people home to avoid a massacre. In his attempt to escape, the king was captured. Since he wanted to serve as a Christian example, he cast down his weapons. When the conditions were once again stipulated by the chief, Edmund refused to officially surrender his kingdom. He would not bow down to their pagan, wicked demands.

The king's refusal infuriated the Danes. They beat him with sticks, tied him to a tree, and tore his flesh with whips. When Edmund appealed to His Lord and King, his captors became more brutal. They shot arrows into him until he looked like a thistle covered with prickles. In spite of the abuse, Edmund would not renounce Christ. The Danish leader finally severed the young king's head with an axe.

Even though King Edmund died in his twenties, he was faithful to his King, Lord, and Savior to the end. He would not let go of his faith to save his own life. He not only made an impression on the people he ruled over and the enemies who threw every form of wickedness at him, but on following generations of people like me who would discover the endearing testimony he left behind. King Edmund was the king who from all appearances grabbed a hold of the Lord's promises with expectation. For, as Jesus promised, if one is willing to lose his or her life for His sake, he or she will gain an eternal, glorious life.

Whosoever therefore shall confess me before men, him will I confess also before my Father which is in heaven. But whosoever shall deny me before men, him will I also deny before my Father, who is in heaven (Matthew 10:32-33).

Strength in Weakness:

Some of the stories in this book such as the previous one about King Edmund, were obtained from Carolyn Wilde's book entitled,

Torchbearers. Another person that Carolyn wrote about was a woman by the name of Annie Taylor. She was born in 1855.

Due to her frail state of having a weak heart, the doctor told her parents to not even bother to educate her. However, we know that God sees weakness as an opportunity to show Himself mighty. Annie became such a vessel. In spite of her frailty, she did live on to receive the Lord Jesus, and was educated in the fields of art and medicine. In fact, she completed twelve years of intensive training in Italy, Germany, and the London Hospital.

When she was young, the Lord had tugged on her heartstrings to be a missionary, but because of her weak physical state she felt she could never finish the course. Besides, the pleas for such missionaries were directed towards the strong and not the weak. However, the heart tug never went away. Finally, she knelt and consecrated herself totally to the Lord. The call to go to Tibet was settled in her spirit. She made plans to obey even in the midst of great outcries against such a notion. She was reminded that Tibet was the highest place in the world with the most rugged and difficult terrain in the world. The only ones who dared to go there were mountain climbers. Annie was aware that a weak heart probably would not survive the high altitude of Tibet, but she maintained her resolve to go, and with a sense of humor added that they need not worry for she had no intention of climbing a 29,000-foot-high mountain.

Her journey began on September 2, 1892. She wore heavy sheepskin and her shelter could be anything from a cave to a tent to a snowdrift. She wrote in her diary that the ground was her bed, the stars her curtain, and the wind pretty bad about her head. Her guide was a known murderer who also was planning her demise. However, she trusted the Lord to be her shield, buckler, and ever-faithful companion. At times she would wake at night gasping for every breath as her heart raced to what appeared to be its expected end. She would beg God to enable her to finish the course set before her. After all, her call and life were a matter of His business.

When she finally arrived at her destination, she shuddered at the heavy spiritual darkness engulfing the people. A cave's midnight hour did not compare to the heavy curtain of spiritual darkness that rested upon the people. All she could do was fling herself into the refuge of her Lord, trusting His strength and power to not only enable her to endure, but flow through her as she served as His living testimony.

At the time, Annie was the only known missionary in Tibet. However, she knew that God made her a majority in the midst of grave demonic darkness. The torch she carried would penetrate the most darkened soul with the reality and hope of the Lord. She loved the people and the people were enamored with her. Crowds thronged her as she painted the Gospel message on story cards, which she would eventually pass out to three thousand people. She also gave out a thousand Tibetan and Chinese Bibles. Some copies made their way to the lamas. She recorded that she had heard that the lamas in all the monasteries were reading the Gospel. She introduced many to Jesus, one at a time, leaving pockets of light to break forth in the midst of a land which once stood in complete darkness.

Christians sometimes forget that they are to serve as lights in great darkness. Sadly, the world clamors for each of us to carry worldly torches that simply glitter from a false glory, but how many Christians recognize the glorious privilege of carrying the torch of God? (TB, 239-243)

Therefore I take pleasure in infirmities, in reproaches, in necessities, in persecutions, in distresses for Christ's sake: for when I am weak, then am I strong (2 Corinthians 12:10).

Bits of History

Who Am I?

It is important to have somewhat of a knowledge about history and those who defined our present-day concept of Christianity, religion, and morality. See how many of the following questions you can answer.

1. This godly saint and teacher was given the task of raising the young man who would succeed Louis XIV to the throne of France.
2. This foremost Baptist minister of the 19th century was a descendant of Edward Winslow, a pilgrim leader who came to the New World on the Mayflower.
3. He was a bishop of Antioch and a personal disciple of the Apostle John. He also was martyred in Rome.
4. This pioneer missionary was given the label of the Wolf from Scotland by the religious people who opposed his work.
5. This preacher from Scotland not only loved his adopted country, the United States of America, but He also served as chaplain to the United States Senate.
6. He was considered one of the most learned Christian teachers of his day. He was also a prolific writer of the pre-Nicene church, dictating around 2,000 works.
7. William Carey, John Wesley, and Murray McCheyne were impressed when they read about the life of this missionary.
8. This Christian writer became a lawyer, but felt called to serve God. He not only pastored churches, but he served as a confederate chaplain after being detained as a prisoner of war for 1½ years in the Federal Prison in St Louis.

9. He wrote various apologies, works directed against heretics, and exhortations in Latin to other Christians. He also appeared to serve as a presbyter in the church at Carthage, North Africa.
10. Along with George Whitefield, this preacher was part of the great awakening. He preached a famous sermon about sinners in the hands of an angry God that is read and studied today. He also greatly influenced David Brainerd.
11. While holding evangelistic meetings in America this evangelist from England sustained serious injuries when he had to jump from the third story window of his hotel after it caught on fire.
12. This reformer was one of the individuals who was instrumental in the repeal of the Stamp Act of 1765.
13. He was the bishop of Milan and has been called the "Father of Latin Hymnody."
14. He was a 16th century scholar and translator who became a leading figure in Protestant reformism.
15. He was considered a careful historian and great scholar. He translated the Bible into Latin—the Vulgate.
16. This Canadian Presbyterian Missionary witnessed great revival in China in the late 1800s.
17. One time tax collector in his native town in North Africa, he became the bishop of Ruspe, but was exiled for many years to Sardinia.
18. This Puritan lived during the execution of Charles I. He was a leader of the Congregationalists and was considered one of the greatest scholars.
19. He was a personal disciple of the Apostle John who served as the bishop of Smyrna. He heroically died a martyr at 86 years of age.
20. This American Presbyterian formed Westminster Theological Seminary after leading a conservative revolt against Modernist theology at Princeton.
21. He was a vigorous opponent of Christianity, but after his conversion he wrote seven books against paganism.
22. These two founding fathers and presidents of the United Stated died on the same day, July 4th, 50 years after the declaration of Independence was first signed.

23. He was one of the first of the great leaders in Africa who explored in his writings the relations between faith and reason.
24. Depending on the subject, this founding father of our nation wrote letters to the editor under various pseudonyms. One of his opponents stated that his pen stung like a horned snake.
25. Third century distinguished lawyer of African origin who had converted to Christianity from Stoicism.

(The answer to these questions can be found on page 250.)

******

Man's Preference

I have been reading about how America was the great experiment to show that man does not need to be ruled by the strong, cruel hand of despotism and tyranny. Granted, man in an unbridled form is the most dangerous and destructive creature there is. Without inner restraint, he will prove the most vile, wretched base depot that could ever be imagined. At such a stage it takes that which is most vile, base, and wretched to rule over such a despicable creature with an iron hand of indifference and hatred. It is for this reason a leader will mirror the attitude of the people, and the people will embrace the leader that represents their inner state.

This brings us to the type of restraint that allows man to rule over himself. What rules over such individuals is righteousness. These people understand that they must be upright in their standing with God, right in the bent of their inner character, and moral and honorable in their conduct towards others. Granted, there will be just laws present. However, these just laws are not present to rule such individuals, for they are subject to a higher and excellent law, but to protect them from those who prefer the base ways of despotism. When you consider those who rage, it is not those who hold to the excellent ways of moral character, but those who resent such restraints.

Those who abhor such restraints will rage against that which holds up a higher standard by their lives. These individuals will accuse those who will not budge from the excellent ways of righteousness of being hateful, mean, and cruel. Yet, they are the ones who are raging, revealing anger, displaying hatred, and proving to be cruel and indifferent. They are the ones who are trying to push their immorality and prejudices on others. They are the ones who want all restraints thrown out no matter how unprotected it leaves others. However, in their foolishness they do not realize that without such restraints, they stand as sitting ducks waiting for the tidal wave of despotism that they have encouraged and nurtured by their many angry affronts against all that is decent, to roll in and destroy them.

Many people have brought out that America's greatness was a matter of its excellent character that was established by moral principles and just laws that were drawn upon by our founding fathers. This fact has been brought out by our founding fathers, as well as others. Consider some of their writings and statements, while examining what our present leadership of despotism tells us about the moral environment that has managed to take center stage in our nation.

- The question is a crucial one for the future of our country. All history bears witness to the fact *there can be no public virtue without private morality.* There cannot be good government except in a good society. And there cannot be a good society unless the majority of individuals in it are at least *trying* to be good people. This is especially true in a democracy, where leaders and representatives are chosen from the people, by the people. The character of a democratic government will never be better than the character of the people it governs. A nation that is traveling the low road is a nation that is self-destructing. It is doomed, sooner or later, to collapse from within, or to be destroyed from without. And not all its wealth, science and technology will be able to save it.

  -Clare Boothe Luce

- History fails to record a single precedent in which nations subject to moral decay have not passed into political and economic decline. There has been either a spiritual awakening to overcome the moral lapse, or a progressive deterioration leading to ultimate national disaster.

-General Douglas MacArthur

- We have no government armed with power capable of contending with human passions unbridled by morality and religion. Avarice, ambition, revenge or gallantry, would break the strongest cords of our Constitution as a whale goes through a net. Our Constitution was made only for a moral and religious people. It is wholly inadequate to the government of any other.

  -John Adams

- Is there no virtue among us? If there be not, we are in a wretched situation. No theoretical checks—no form of government can render us secure. To suppose that any form of government will secure liberty or happiness without any virtue in the people, is a chimerical idea.

  -James Madison

- Only a virtuous people are capable of freedom. As nations become corrupt and vicious, they have more need of masters.

  -Benjamin Franklin

- Of all the disposition and habits which lead to political prosperity, religion and morality are indispensable supports…It is substantially true that virtue or morality is a necessary spring of popular government. The rule, indeed, extends with more or less force to every species of free government.

  -George Washington

******

- If we are not governed by God, then we will be ruled by tyrants.

  -William Penn

- People take much stock in their philosophies, facts, and understanding of history. However, philosophy that *lacks a proper context* will produce hypocrites, facts that *are not in context* prove to be foolish, and history *taken out of context* becomes nothing more than wicked indoctrination.

-RJK

❖ And, for the support of this declaration, with a firm reliance on the protection of Divine Providence, we mutually pledge to each other our lives, our fortunes, and our sacred honor.

-Signers of the Declaration of Independence

❖ Why then, sir, do we longer delay? Why still deliberate? Let this happy day give birth to an American republic! Let her arise, not to devastate and conquer, but to re-establish the reign of peace and law. The eyes of Europe are fixed upon us; she demands of us a living example of freedom, that may exhibit a contrast, in the felicity of the citizen, to the ever-increasing tyranny which desolates her polluted shores. She invites us to prepare an asylum, where the unhappy may find solace, and the persecuted repose. She entreats us to cultivate a propitious soil, where that genuine plant, which first sprang and grew in England, but is now withered by the blasts of Scottish tyranny, may revive and flourish, sheltering under its salubrious and interminable shade all the unfortunate of the human race. If we are not this day wanting in our duty to our country, the names of the American legislators of '76 will be placed by posterity at the side of those of Theseus, of Lycurgus, of Romula, of Numa, of the three Williams of Nassau, and of all those whose memory has been, and forever will be, dealt to virtuous men and good citizens.

-Richard Henry Lee
Speech in favor of passing a resolution to dissolve all political connection with Great Britain in 1776

****

Words From Samuel Adams (Founding Father)

I had a limited understanding on most matters concerning the real core of this country's history. Granted, I knew about Christopher Columbus, the Pilgrims, and the Revolutionary and Civil Wars. However, due to the abuses of our present leaders, it has become important for me to get back to the real foundation of our country. Many of our founding fathers were men who sought inspired wisdom from above. As a result, they became steadfast in their principles and beliefs. They believed that if a country was founded on the moral principles of God, and governed by the just Laws of heaven, that it would come forth in excellence. They understood that before new life could come out of anything there had to be a time of travailing, struggle, and conflict. One of the men that caught my attention was Samuel Adams. In the book about his life, author Ira Stoll brings this man to life to once again to speak to the moral conscience of men about matters that are essential in maintaining the quality of life. The thing that fascinated me the most about Samuel Adams is that he effectively fought the Revolutionary War with ink and pen.

Here are some of his sayings.

- Liberty: The choicest gift that Heaven has lent to man.
- Neither the wisest constitution nor the wisest laws will secure the liberty and happiness of a people whose manners are universally corrupt.
- Is it not High Time for the People of this Country explicitly to declare, whether they will be Freemen or Slaves? It is an important Question which ought to be decided. It concerns us more than any Thing in this Life. The Salvation of our Souls is interested in the Event: For wherever Tyranny is establish'd, Immorality of every Kind comes in like a Torrent. It is in the interest of Tyrants to reduce the people to Ignorance and Vice. For they cannot live in any Country where Virtue and Knowledge prevail. The Religion and public Liberty of a People are intimately connected; their Interests are interwoven, they cannot subsist separately; and therefore they rise and fall together. For this Reason, it is always

observable, that those who are combined to destroy the People's Liberties, practice every Art to poison their Morals. How greatly then does it concern us, at all Events, to put a Stop to the Progress of Tyranny.

- If taxes are laid upon us in any shape without our having a legal representation where they are laid, are we not reduced from the character of free subjects to the miserable state of tributary slaves?
- For true patriots to be silent, is dangerous.
- The liberties of our country, the freedom of our civil Constitution, are worth defending at all hazards; and it is our duty to defend them against all attacks. We have received them as a fair inheritance from our worthy ancestors: they purchased them for us with toil and danger and expense of treasure and blood, and transmitted them to us with care and diligence. It will bring an everlasting mark of infamy on the present generation, enlightened as it is, if we should suffer them to be wrested from us by violence without a struggle or to be cheated out of them by the artifices of false and designing men.
- The cloak of Christianity is the threadbare garb of hypocrisy.
- He who can flatter a despot, or be flattered by him, without feeling the remonstrances of his own mind against it, may be remarkable for the guise and appearance of sanctity, but he has very little if any true religion—If he habitually allows himself in it, he is a hardened impenitent sinner against GOD and COUNTRY.
- Whether America shall long preserve her Freedom or not, will depend on her Virtue.
- While the People are virtuous they cannot be subdued; but when once they lose their Virtue they will be ready to surrender their Liberties to the first *external* or *internal* Invader.

Stand fast therefore in the liberty with which Christ hath made us free, and be not entangled again with the yoke of bondage (Galatians 5:1).

❖ God hasn't given up on this country, which is His latest experiment in human freedom and opportunity.

-Peter Marshall
(JMM, pg. 46)

- Those who profess to favor freedom and yet depreciate agitation, are people who want crops without plowing the ground; they want rain without thunder and lighting; they want the ocean without the roar of its many waters. The struggle may be a moral one, or it may be a physical one, or it may be both. But it must be a struggle. Power concedes nothing without a demand; it never has and it never will

  -Frederick Douglass

- We on this continent should never forget that men first crossed the Atlantic not to find soil for their ploughs but to secure liberty for their souls.

  -Robert J. McCracken

- Posterity: you will never know how much it has cost my generation to preserve your freedom. I hope you will make good use of it.

  -John Quincy Adams

- The essence of modern dictatorship is the combination of one-dimensional, flat thinking with power and terror.

  -Theodore Haecker

******

When asked which person left the most permanent impression on history, British writer, H.G. Wells replied that judging a person's greatness by historical standards: "By this test, Jesus stands first."

"I am a historian, I am not a believer, but I must confess as a historian that this penniless preacher from Nazareth is irrevocably the very center of history. Jesus Christ is easily the most dominant figure in all history."

And whosoever shall fall on this stone shall be broken: but on whosoever it shall fall, it will grind him to powder (Matthew 21:44).

- Certain individuals have tried to hijack President Ronald Reagan's legacy as a man and a leader. In an interview with Reagan's speech writer who wrote the famous speech about bringing the Berlin Wall down, he summarized the source behind Reagan's leadership. He stated that Ronald Reagan was great because he was right. The speech writer shared how Reagan knew the speech about bringing the Berlin wall down would set many of his team on edge, but he knew he had to do it because it was the right thing to do.

******

Soldiers with Petticoats

The birth of a nation involves travailing of great proportions. When we think of the birth of this nation, we think of George Washington. The sacrifices for some were immense. Many times, when we think of greatness, we overlook the women who suffered, and the children who tasted great loss.

When we think of those who literally fought for this nation's right to exist as a sovereign nation, we think of the men, but the reality is that women fought alongside the men. One such woman was Margaret Corbin. She followed her husband into battle. He manned the cannons and when he was fatally wounded, she took his place, firing the cannon until she also was severely wounded. Three years later, she became the first woman in the United States to receive a pension from Congress.

Another woman was Deborah Sampson. She actually impersonated a man so she could fight in the Revolutionary War. She took part in combats and skirmishes along with the men. When a musket ball hit her in the thigh, she tended to it herself to keep her secret. However, her secret was eventually unveiled when she came down with malignant fever. She received equal payment as the men and received a pension.

Women also served as spies during the Revolutionary War, alerting American troops concerning the enemies' various movements. General Washington picked Ann Simpson Davis to carry messages to his generals while the army was in eastern Pennsylvania. She later received a letter of commendation from Washington for her services.

We often note men for their great service, but where would we be without silent souls such as women?

Revival on a US Warship

The year was 1857. The battleship USS North Carolina, a 74-gun ship of the line launched in 1820 at the Philadelphia Naval Yard, was anchored in New York harbor. Her long years of duty were now reduced to being a naval receiving ship.

Among the many sailors on board were four young Christian crewmen, who decided that they should meet and pray. Looking for a private place for prayer, they met on the lower deck. Falling upon their knees, they instantly were filled with the Presence of God. So great was their joy that they started to sing and praise the Lord.

Wicked sailors, who were upon the top deck, heard the jubilant singing and decided to investigate. Upon discovering that it was coming from a secret prayer meeting, the vile bunch decided to mock and jeer. Descending the iron stairs to the place of prayer, the mob fell under the powerful presence of the Holy Spirit. Their jeers turned to bitter tears. Conviction overcame them and they began to cry out to God for mercy and forgiveness. For several days, the prayer meeting continued. Hundreds of the crew were converted. The captain of the ship sent a message ashore requesting the help of pastors and ministers to come and pray with the sailors.

The USS North Carolina became a bastion of revival. Converted sailors, upon completing their training, were assigned to other ships in the fleet. Wherever they went, revival broke out. Revival swept the US fleet. Prayer is a powerful force!

-Michael Edds

******

Jerusalem and the Temple

Jerusalem is the city of the great and coming King, the Lord Jesus Christ. The Lord chose this city. It is considered the spiritual center of the earth and is mentioned 1,000 times in the Scriptures.

"Jerusalem" means the city of peace. Clearly, its history proves contrary and even today it serves as a "cup of trembling" to the whole world.

According to Ruth Specter Lascelle in her book *Jewish Faith and the New Covenant,* Jerusalem is a city that has been the most sacked. Historical records show that it has been besieged 47 times, resulting in it being completely brought to the ground 17 times. These figures translate that approximately once every 75 years it has been encompassed by enemy armies, and once every 200 years it has been left in ruins. We know that today many leaders are eying Jerusalem.

In the near future these leaders will cause their armies to encompass Jerusalem. In the end, the Lord will destroy these enemies of Israel, and as the true King of Jerusalem, He will reclaim the throne of David. He will cause all matters to become new as He purges with righteous judgment and restores what has been ordained by Him.

One of those things that will be completely restored is the temple. The temple identifies Jerusalem as the spiritual center of the earth. It signifies God's dwelling place among men. King David wanted to build the first temple, but because he was a man of war it was passed down to his son, Solomon. This dwelling place of God had to be a magnificent structure. It took seven years to build it. According to 1955 figures before inflation it was calculated that it would cost over 87 million dollars just for the materials and the food for workmen. Can you imagine what it would cost to build it today?

In his article in the May-June 2011 issue of, "Zion's Fire," Kevin Howard stated that according to present day figures, the gold and silver alone used in the building of Solomon's temple would easily top $218 billion in value. He pointed out that 22½ tons of pure gold was used just in the Holy of Holies. He compared the value of these precious metals to the most costly natural disaster of Katrina, which cost this country $80 billion dollars. He also gave the example of an employee that earned $25/hr. It would take this worker *three million* years, working seven days a week with tax-free wages to earn $218 billion dollars. As the Word states, this was a magnificent building that would stand distinct among all other buildings.

However, we know that man now serves as the temple of God. We are told that what beautifies man, making him a magnificent and worthy residence for God, is humility that has been tempered and brought forth by meekness.

For the LORD taketh pleasure in his people: he will beautify the meek with salvation (Psalms 149:4).

A Bit of Nostalgia

The papers were yellow from age. I carefully held them in my hand, almost afraid to loosen them from the hold of the rubber band, concerned that they would crumble into pieces. My friend, Larry Human heard about my fascination with past eras. He had told me about papers that had been passed down to him from his mother, and had kindly asked me if I would be interested in examining them. I just could not turn down such an opportunity.

These papers dated from 1878 through 1937. The bundle contained letters, land deeds, leases, and even old tally sheets of groceries and railroad cars. Even though the people who wrote them were complete strangers to me, I was aware that they lived. It was clear that they did not live on credit, but lived within their means because the grocery lists were accompanied by how much each item cost. Needless to say, the addition was done in long hand.

There were other little interesting facts as well. Perhaps the fact that it had cost $5.00 to make a copy of a picture, honey had been sold for some money, or that the cotton crop had yielded 132 bales would probably bring a boring sigh from many. However, these people had hopes, dreams, and challenges. It is true that in the scheme of things their lives would not seem important to anyone else; however, each generation exists because of those who have gone on before us. We now experience the fruits of their innovation, hard work, sacrifices, and determination.

The truth is I would not be here, nor would you if hearty souls such as these had not lived. There would be no history if these individuals had not made some type of mark. These marks allow us to see into another time. We would all like to think that it was a more innocent time, or that we presently live in a far better advanced age.

Were the times simpler in the late 1800s and early 1900s? It was interesting to study the stamps. The oldest letters had a two-cent stamp on them, but there was one that had a three-cent stamp. It only cost one penny to mail a postcard. The two-cent stamps had a picture of a woman on it. However, there was also a picture of President Harding on one of the stamps and another stamp depicting Columbus discovering America.

There were a couple of different official documents that caught my attention. The first one was a selective service card. Of course, there was no picture of the person, but the weight and height were written in along with the fact that he had a scar on his head. Otherwise, there were boxes marked that indicated the person's origins, hair, and eye color. He was a white male who was 5'7" tall, weighed 154 pounds, had blue eyes, black hair, and a ruddy completion.

Another interesting document was what appeared to be a carbon copy of a typed letter. It was not the neatest type I have ever seen, but it was in the era when people were moving into new inventions such as manual typewriters. The letter was from a bank. At the top of the printed stationary the bank touted that its capital and surplus was a whole whopping $60,000.00. The letter recognized that the person was having a difficult time of paying off his note for $165.00. The bank was reminding the individual that it could only renew his loan once, and after that action would have to be taken.

Although not an official document, there was a letter written with a quill pen from an executer of an estate. Apparently, Mr. John Brown had deceased and let his wishes be known. He had left his remaining estate to be divided between the named benefactors. After the division was made and the fees paid to the executer, the beneficiary's portion who received this letter was $37.40.

The land deeds were interesting to study. There were three different deeds securing certain property for only one dollar. Whether it was a transaction between family or friends it is hard to say. The other deeds for land indicated that parcels of land could be purchased from $35.00 up to $210.00. The largest amount of $1,600.00 was paid out to obtain a gas lease.

The most insight into the lives of these people was gained from reading their personal letters. Clearly, the letters that served as their main means of communication would appear archaic to the present generation, but you could see the personal touch along with substance, quality, and self-respect. Most of the letters were written in pencil, but I recognized the lined yellowish paper from when I was a first grader. The paper had lasting qualities and the envelopes were made of sturdy material. The letters were written between family members who lived in Texas, Oklahoma, and Arkansas. The names attached to these letters were typical, such as Peck, Brown, and Hill. The recipients of the letters usually spoke of the pleasure of receiving such correspondence. Even though there were times they could only drop a few lines, you could tell they did not want to lose touch with each other.

Like most typical letters for that day, they spoke of family happenings, the weather, the crops, and occasionally allowed an opinion, judgment, or a bit of gossip to peek out from the pages. Many started out with a thankful attitude that they had received previous correspondences, and they always ended in a warm, but formal way. For example, one such writer would end with, "Your loving Daughter", but she would sign her complete name.

Needless to say, the health and activities of the family took center stage. There was the grandson who had a terrible boil on his wrist that was quite bothersome. There was also the part about baby Nelly who was as "fat as a pig and nearly walking".

Occasionally there was a bit of competition. According to one letter the girls in Oklahoma were more attractive than those in Texas. However, one letter bragged that the dirt in Texas was very black and rich. To add to competition there was a bit of matchmaking. According to one writer, he had picked out a fellow for a woman named Maggie. The guy was a perfect match, especially since he was a doctor. There was also the part about going to church. The writer noted that those who attended were dressed well and riding and driving good horses.

It was obvious that these people had a foundation of faith. There were references to the Lord's blessing. One writer stated that if the good Lord would let them live, that next year they would be able to see the fruits of their labor.

Regardless of what era I study there is one continual factor when it comes to God and man, and that is nothing changes. Times can change, but man finds himself in need of God's intervention. The times may become advanced, but all blessings still find their origins in an unchanging God. Regardless of the era man lives in, he will always find himself a part of the cycle of life. He is born, lives, and dies. However, if God is not part of the equation, man remains void of hope. He can strive to possess the world, but will die empty and spiritually bankrupt.

I have learned that life possesses seasons and cycles to remind each of us that our time on earth will prove to be short. As a result, we must come to terms with the whys' as to the purpose of our present life. It is up to each of us to acquire and pass on a heritage, regardless of how long we may live on this earth.

There are different types of heritages, but the greatest one we must pass down is the spiritual one. Without the heritage to identify us to God's redemption, any hope of ensuring a future for the next generation will meet a tragic end as it will find itself consumed in judgment.

What kind of heritage are you leaving? Will it cause nostalgia, or will it be consumed by the judgment that abides upon the foolish ways of the wicked?

And as it is appointed unto men once to die, but after this the judgment (Hebrews 9:27).

******

A Journey Through Time

If you were to get a sense of history during a certain time or age, the quickest way would be to study the art, music, and entertainment that were emerging during that period. These sources serve as valuable mirrors into the souls of people. They give insight into the environment, attitude, and prevalent spirit of that particular period. If you don't believe me, consider the works of Shakespeare and Charles Dickens, while comparing them to the present works. The backdrops signify the environment, while the attitudes the spirit, and the emphasis in regard to life, love, country, and God, the prevailing moral climate of each age.

Granted, there is one thing that never changes and that is the struggles of man and the moral issues that confront him, but the backdrops in which he expresses and contends with the issues of life vary. Such variation causes each generation to perceive that its problems or struggles are unique. Due to great ignorance about the past, it appears that each generation fails to discern that its particular environment is, nothing more than a window dressing that simply covers what the real truth about such matters is and what remains consistent regardless of the times.

As you study each trend, you begin to see how the worldview, the perceptions, and psychology of people are being influenced by the different forms of art that is being produced. One wonders if such trends occur because people are changing or whether it is being orchestrated by those who want to influence culture in a certain way. The truth is most people are like sheep. They do not determine the trends; rather, trends are the waves that end up carrying them in a certain direction, thereby, affecting their attitudes and behavior.

These waves are created by those who are pulling the strings behind the scenes. These individuals are like the Wizard of Oz. It is all an image, but they know how to present it in such a way that people actually lay claim to it as being their reality. They do not know they are being managed much like puppets on the end of strings. The truth is the arts often become a means of propaganda. It sets up powerful images that will create a certain reality in which people are seduced and conditioned to believe that it is who they are, or that is the way a matter must be. It will not only influence people's worldview, but it will determine their attitude about matters, the tastes they prefer, and their moral sense.

I discovered this fact when I did an outline about the trends of music to show how we are influenced by the world. It was my goal to show that we are not where we are as a society because we are more intelligent, wise, or clever, but because the powers to be are conditioning us. Granted, these influences may not be bad, but they can prove to be unrealistic, causing frustration, disillusionment, and anger that end in complete rejection of what is right and true altogether. The key is the same, what fruits are such environments producing?

I was born in 1955. My uncles were in their teenage years when I was first aware of the power behind lyrics and music that were catching the fancy of the unharnessed energy of the youth. I slightly remember some of the hair styles, types of dress, and attitudes. Therefore, when I watched TV series such as "Happy Days" and movies that depict that time, nostalgia would often sweep over me. I would think to myself, "Now those were the days!" However, were they "the days", or did they represent a time to me that did not appear to be insane?

Today I believe we are living in precarious times, but we did not get here overnight. We have been conditioned by each succeeding wave of indoctrination that has swept the previous generation. Each generation has been sold a bill of goods, but each package has been laced with the poison that has been prepared for that particular generation, desensitizing the people as to the purpose and agenda behind the conditioning.

As I consider the era of 1950 to present, I can see that each generation has been conditioned to embrace greater insanity. The reality of arts is that there is an unrealistic, silly side that causes what is real, necessary, or decent to be considered unobtainable or foolish to those who come to a place of despair and hopelessness. The TV shows of the 50's showed family values and decency, but it did so in light of comedy. There is nothing funny about the problems that confront families; therefore, it made the concept of family values unrealistic. The 1950's were also the era of love songs that were attractive but not realistic.

Such an environment causes disillusionment. This brings us to the other contrast of the 1950's, "Rock and Roll" music. "Rock and Roll" music was touted as being a form of self-expression. It was a declaration of independence from that which was considered "fantasy" to that which was exciting. However, such independence encourages selfishness, where a person must keep his or her self-serving preferences in order to avoid being identified to that which was out of touch.

Out of this independence grew a mistrust for all authority. Such mistrust breeds anger towards that which proves to be disappointing. Needless to say, the Viet Nam Conflict escalated the environment. Since Socialist philosophies were taking center stage in the colleges, the inexperienced youth were primed to partake of the deadly seeds of the ideology of Communism. Since the youth was primed to declare independence, they would go one step further, they would fiercely resist the establishment altogether. They would deem it all stupid, unrealistic, and a lie. They would chase after anything that would free them from the grave, unrealistic bondage put on them by the establishment of family and government. They would throw all values out, mock any decency, and fling themselves into anything that would dull them to what they considered to be the hypocritical presentation of the wretched institution. If is for this reason that the music in the 1960's had some type of message in it. Many times, it revealed sorrow born out of disappointment, but such sorrow also became the means for justifying the anger that was taking center stage in lawlessness and rebellion.

The resistance against the establishment left a big gaping hole that had to be filled with something. The 1960's had revealed that it did not matter what you pursue, it would eventually prove to be all vanity. It would always leave you empty, unfulfilled, and utterly dissatisfied.

This is the environment that greeted the 1970's. The 1960's left many unresolved issues. Songs with hidden messages came forth in the 1970's, revealing how lost the upcoming generation had become because there were no stable roots. It was as if nothing mattered for the attitude was "anything goes." Everything seemed perverted by the escalation of drugs, and all appeared hopeless because there were no real boundaries. As a result, hard rock made its great appearance as everything was being screamed in time with beats that could hypnotize the listeners into nirvana—a state of nothingness.

The emptiness of the 1970's left a spiritual vacuum. The conditioning of the 1950's and 1960's, produced an environment where there were no absolutes; therefore, that which was considered fundamental was being mocked. Everything had become relative. The defiance that was finding its momentum in the past couple of generations, manifested itself in an utter restlessness. The generation coming to maturity in the 1980's was like waves on the ocean. The youth were not sure where to go; therefore, they went into extremes in music. This is when the hard-core metal rock could be heard blaring out of speakers in an attempt to silence the emptiness of it all.

In the 1990's, the screaming gave way to a new form of art: Rap. Rap was a way of getting the message of disillusionment, skepticism, and hatred out on the airwaves. In rap all there needed to be was rhythm, beat, allowing a person to step to the cadence call of the particular message.

As each generation digressed into the next environment, most discernment went out the backdoor. Since all boundaries were mocked, godly values rejected, justice disregarded, and moral decency considered inferior, tolerance for everything and anything was advocated; except in the case of where there was no tolerance or adjustment to a matter. Rebellion at this stage became a platform for extreme revolutionary sentiment. If you don't agree with me, you will be considered dispensable. If you cannot promote my cause, you are not worthy to breathe the same air or take up any space.

This brings us to a new decade. It is clear that the deadly seeds being planted and cultivated for the last five decades are coming to fruition. The results are frightening. The reality is that this decade may very well signal the end to the insanity that has been coming to fruition for decades in this country. The end is obvious, it will be death. After all, the tree that produces deadly fruit can only result in death. There is no life to be found in any of it.

This brings me to another subject. The music in churches also reveals how much of the world has influenced it. This music is to attract the fleshly side, not to spiritually challenge, inspire, and establish people on the sure foundation of Jesus Christ. When people have chided me for my narrow view about the type of music that should be used in worship, I remember what my co-laborer Jeannette used to say, "Would we hear such music played before the throne of God?"

Music does have a spirit and purpose behind. It is a powerful medium and avenue that Satan has used effectively. This should not surprise us since Ezekiel 28:12-15 tells us that Satan was an anointed cherub whose workmanship was that of music.

The quality of our present is being determined by what we expose ourselves to. The arts, whether it comes in the form of the art, music, and entertainment conditions us. It is often loaded with propaganda. Keep in mind all propaganda has a self-serving agenda. The question we must ask ourselves is what do our preferences tell about our own souls. Will it reveal that we are silly because of the fairy-tale environment we insist on? Will people see the angry side of rebellion, the self-serving side of indifference, or the dark side of destruction in our attitudes and ways?

Jesus was clear that we can know where our type of life is coming from. We can know whether our fruit speaks of life or death. We can know and must know if we are going to survive the days we are living in. The fruits are the only sure test as to whether something is pulsating with life, or whether death reigns in and through it.

A good tree cannot bring forth evil fruit, neither can a corrupt tree bring forth good fruit. Every tree that bringeth not forth good fruit is hewn down, and cast into the fire. Wherefore by their fruits ye shall know them (Matthew 7:18-20).

ANSWER TO PUZZLE

John	David	Zacchaeus	Amos	Nimrod	Mark
Paul	Demas	Joshua	Joab	Cain	James
Abel	Adam	Peter	Titus	Ahab	Judas
Lot	Simon	Dan	Silas	Herod	Amos
Eli	Hadad	Saul	Ham	Barnabas	
Job	Eve	Hosea	Mary	Dorcus	

A man named John had various abandoned creatures he cared for at a farm outside of an unincorporated place called Pauley, located in Jameson County. In the beginning the various animals kept everything in somewhat of a chaotic state; therefore, he called the place Babel. However, in time he had developed procedures that made a lot of improvements, as well as eliminated many challenges. As a result, he felt accomplished in his job. Even his wife, Ada videoed the various measures they both had instituted to help the place to run smoothly. It was obvious to any onlooker that they made mass improvements. It was so fined-tuned that Ada made special food for exotic creatures such as their snake, Lulu and a mouthy parrot named Simon to save money and ensure their health. Clearly, the couple had added to the quality of the lives of the creatures entrusted to their care. However, on this particular day, John had an omniscient feeling. Unknowingly, it would be a day he would mark down in his journal as being insightful. Like always, he took the time to clean and hose all the different cages of the creatures entrusted to him. He also took note that at least the orphan cats, Zacchaeus was comfortably resting on his normal perch, and Joshua had once again secured his preferred place on the old chair. As he absent mindedly leaned down to pet, Ernest his dog, he became aware of a stir in the barn. A bash incident was clearly occurring. He rushed to the scene to see with consternation that his snake was on the loose. Usually, the snake, Lulu, kept low key, but at other times her odd and unpredictable mannerisms made her a Judas. This time her activities appeared as if she was causing a major danger to the order of the facility. She had somehow slipped out of her glass case and was making an assault on the cage of the rabbit, Maryjo. From John's immediate summation of the situation, it was obvious that a most interesting set of events were quickly being set into motion. The snake was actually attempting to wrap herself around the cage of the anxious rabbit. Clearly, Maryjo abhorred Lulu seeing her as a possible meal. Even though the wire kept her protected from the assault, it ushered panic into the midst of the barn. Maryjo's excited state was causing the hamster, Dorcus to spin her wheel out of control in her cage, causing her cage to fall off of the table. The sound of the cage inspired the squirrel, Nimrod to burrow a hole in the straw, and the skunk, Cain, to turn his posterior to the whole fiasco. Since the snake was trying to put the squeeze on the rabbit, the raccoon, Ahab was taking the opportunity to eye the goldfish, Basil as it was swimming in a make-shift pond near by. Before he could save Maryjo, resurrect Dorcus' cage, uncover Nimrod from his hiding place, turn Cain in the right direction, remove Ahab from temptation, and pull Basil out of the possible jaws of death, John had to subdue the instigator behind the chaos. As he unwrapped Lulu from the cage, he began to wonder about his procedures. If one snake can throw everything into chaos in a matter of seconds, what does it say about the real plans and intelligence of mankind? Perhaps our first parents in the Garden of Eden could easily answer that question.

Answers to the Questions Who am I?

1. Fenelon
2. Octavius Winslow
3. Ignatius
4. Dr. Robert Reid Kalley
5. Peter Marshall
6. Origen
7. David Brainerd
8. E. M. Bounds
9. Tertullian
10. Jonathan Edwards
11. Leonard Ravenhill
12. George Whitefield
13. Ambrose of Milan
14. William Tyndall
15. Jerome
16. Jonathan Goforth
17. Fulgence of Ruspe
18. John Owen
19. Polycarp
20. J. Greshem Machen
21. Arnobius
22. J. Adams & T. Jefferson
23. Clement of Alexandria
24. Samuel Adams
25. Marcus Minucius Felix

Bibliography

(FRG) Finding the Reality of God, © 1989 by Paris W. Reidhead, Bible Teaching Ministries, Inc.

(GPQ) The Golden Treasury of Patristic Quotations, From 50-750 A.D. © 1996 by I. D. E. Thomas

(DCB) A Dictionary of Early Christian Beliefs, © 1998 by David W. Bercot,Hendrickson Publishers, Inc.

(JMM) Mr. Jones Meet the Master, Sermons and Prayers of Peter Marshall, © 1950, Fleming H. Revell Company

(CHL) The Christian's Secret of a Happy Life, Hannah Whitall Smith, © 1952, Fleming H. Revell Company

(RPR) Revival Pray, Leonard Ravenhill, © 1962, Bethany House Publishers

(WOP) The Weapon of Prayer, E. M. Bounds, © 1997, Whitaker House

(PP) Purpose of Prayer, E. M. Bounds, © 1997, Whitaker House

(ST) Sin and Temptation, from the works of John Owen, © by James M. Huston, Bethany House Publishers

(LDD) The Life and Diary of David Brainerd, © 1949 by Moody Bible Institutes, reprinted 1989 by Baker Books

(SOA) Shadow of the Almighty, © 1958 by Elisabeth Elliot, Harper and Row Publishers

(TB) Torchbearers, Carolyn Wilde, © 1994 by Paul and Carolyn Wilde, Solid Rock Books, Inc.

(CA) God's Goal, Christ as All in All, © 1996 by Manfred Haller, Published by The SeedSowers

(TWG) Talking with God, Francois Fenelon, © 1997 by The Community of Jesus, Inc.

(SH) The Seeking Heart, Francois Fenelon, © 1992 by Christian Book Publication.

(WRP) Will Receive Power, William Law, © by Whitaker House

(PDC) Puritan Daily Devotional Chronicles, © 1195 by I.D. E. Thomas, Hearthstone Publishing, Ltd.

(HFG) Hymns for the Family of God, © 1976 by Pargon Associates, Inc. 1976

(FCB) Faith's Checkbook, C. I. Spurgeon, © 1992 by Whitaker House

(MP) All the Messianic Prophecies of the Bible, © 1973 by Herbert Lockyer, Zondervan

(LC) Full Life in Christ, Andrew Murray, © 2000 by Whitaker House

(DEG) Daily Experience with God, Andrew Murray, © 1984 by Whitaker House

The Wolf from Scotland, William B. Forsyth, © by Evangelical Press, 1988

Great Bible Women of China, Paul Estabrooks, © 1997, Open Doors With Brother Andrews, Inc.

Jewish Faith and the New Covenant, © 1980 by Ruth Specter Lascelle

Prayer Warriors, © 1998 by Christian Publication, Inc.

Seven Miracles that Saved America, Chris Stewart and Ted Steward, © 2009, The Shipley Group and Brian T. Stewart.

Galatians (Commentary), H. A. Ironside, Fifteen Printing, Lorzeaux Brothers

Acts (Commentary), H. A. Ironside, Eighteenth Printing, Lorzeaux Brothers

Understanding the Difficult Words of Jesus, David Bivin and Roy B. Blizzard, © 1983, Makor Foundation

Samuel Adams A Life, © 2008 by Ira Stoll, Free Press

Other books by Rayola Kelley:

Hidden Manna (Original)
Battle for the Soul
Stories of the Heart
Transforming Love & Beyond
The Great Debate
Post to Post: (1) Establishing the Way
Post to Post: (2) Walking in the Way
Post to Post: (3) Meditations Along the Way

Volume One: Establishing Our Life in Christ
My Words are Spirit and Life
The Anatomy of Sin
The Principles of the Abundant Life
The Place of Covenant
Unmasking the Cult Mentality

Volume Two: Putting on the Life of Christ
He Actually Thought it Not Robbery
Revelation of the Cross
In Search of Real Faith
Think on These Things
Follow the Pattern

Volume Three: Developing a Godly Environment
Godly Discipline
Prayer and Worship
Don't Touch That Dial
Face of Thankfulness
ABC's of Christianity

Volume Four: Issues of the Heart
Hidden Manna (Revised)
Bring Down the Sacred Cows
The Manual for the Single Christian Life
Parents are People Too

Volume Five: Challenging the Christian Life
The Issues of Life
Presentation of the Gospel
For the Purpose of Edification
Whatever Happened to the Church?
Women's Place in the Kingdom of God

Volume Six: Developing Our Christian Life
The Many Faces of Christianity
Possessing Our Souls
Experiencing the Christian Life
The Power of Our Testimonies
The Victorious Journey

Volume Seven: Discovering True Ministry
From Prisons and Dots to Christianity
So You Want To Be In Ministry

Devotions
Devotions of the Heart: Books One and Two
Daily Food for the Soul: Books One and Two

Gentle Shepherd Ministries Devotion Series:
Being a Child of God
Disciplining the Strength of our Youth
Coming to Full Age

Nugget Books:
Nuggets From Heaven
Heavenly Gems
More Heavenly Gems
Heavenly Treasures

Gentle Shepherd Ministries Series:

The Christian Life Series
What Matter Is This?
The Challenge of It
The Reality of It
The Leadership Series
Overcoming
A Matter of Authority and Power
The Dynamics of True Leadership

Other Books By:
Jeannette Haley

Books co-authored with Rayola Kelley:
Hidden Manna (original)
The Many Faces of Christianity (Volume 6)
Discovering True Ministry: Volume 7
Post to Post 3: Meditations Along the Way
Other Books:
The Pig and I
Reflections of Wonder (Devotional)
Children's Books:
Little Stories for Little People
Traveler's Tales
The Adventures of Zack and Mira
The Adventures of Paul and Dana
(A House on the Beach)
The Monster of Mystery Valley